P9-DVQ-497

SECOND EDITION

Neil J. Anderson

ACTIVE
Skills for **Reading**: Book 3

HEINLE
CENGAGE Learning

Australia • Brazil • Japan • Korea • Mexico • Singapore • Spain • United Kingdom • United States

**Active Skills for Reading,
2nd Edition Student Book 3**
Neil J. Anderson

Director of Content Development: Anita Raducanu
Director of Product Marketing: Amy Mabley
Editorial Manager: Sean Bermingham
Development Editor: Derek Mackrell
Content Project Manager: Tan Jin Hock
International Marketing Manager: Ian Martin
Sr. Print Buyer: Mary Beth Hennebury
Contributing Writers: Paul MacIntyre and Tay Lesley
Compositor: CHROME Media Pte. Ltd.
Cover/Text Designer: CHROME Media Pte. Ltd.
Printer: Transcontinental
Cover Images: All photos from Photos.com, except amusement park (Index Open) and cyclist (iStockphoto)
Photo Credits
Photos.com: pages 8, 9, 11, 23 (top left and center), 35 (top left), 37, 42, 54, 69 (top row), 71, 97, 105, 115, 117, 122, 123, 127, 129, 134, 143, 146, 151, 161, 163, 186; Landov: pages 13, 29, 30, 57, 64, 94, 100, 173, 192; iStockphoto: pages 18, 23 (bottom row and top right), 25, 47, 48, 51, 69 (bottom row), 76, 81 (top left and bottom), 83, 98, 140, 180, 189; The Kobal Collection: pages 41, 175; Reuters: page 110; Index Open: page 168

Copyright © 2009 by Heinle Cengage Learning

ALL RIGHTS RESERVED. No part of this work covered by the copyright herein may be reproduced, transmitted, stored or used in any form or by any means graphic, electronic, or mechanical, including but not limited to photocopying, recording, scanning, digitizing, taping, Web distribution, information networks, or information storage and retrieval systems, except as permitted under Section 107 or 108 of the 1976 United States Copyright Act, without the prior written permission of the publisher.

For permission to use material from this text or product, submit all requests online at **www.cengage.com/permissions**
Further permissions questions can be emailed to **permissionrequest@cengage.com**

ISBN-13: 978-1-4240-0211-5

ISBN-10: 1-4240-0211-7

Heinle Cengage Learning
25 Thomson Place
Boston, Massachusetts 02210
USA

Cengage Learning is a leading provider of customized learning solutions with office locations around the globe, including Singapore, the United Kingdom, Australia, Mexico, Brazil and Japan. Locate our local office at: **international.cengage.com/region**

Cengage Learning products are represented in Canada by Nelson Education, Ltd.

Visit Heinle online at **elt.heinle.com**
Visit our corporate website at **www.cengage.com**

Printed in Canada
4 5 6 7 8 9 10   11 10

Dedication & Acknowledgments

This book is dedicated to Benjamin Anderson. You will develop into a competent, fluent reader of good books as you read with your parents and family.

ACTIVE Skills for Reading has been a wonderful project to be involved with. I have enjoyed talking with teachers who use the series. I enjoy talking with students who have read passages from the book. When we published the first edition, I had no idea that we would be preparing the second edition so quickly. The success of the book is due to the teachers and students who have been engaged in ACTIVE reading. To the readers of ACTIVE Skills for Reading, I thank you.

I also express great appreciation to Paul MacIntyre for your significant contributions to this edition. It is a great pleasure to work with a committed professional like you. I also express appreciation to Derek Mackrell, Sean Bermingham, and Chris Wenger from Thomson. The support you provided me was unbelievable. I enjoy working with you. Special thanks to Maria O'Conor who played an essential role in the conception of the first edition of ACTIVE Skills for Reading.

Neil J. Anderson

Reviewers for this edition

Chiou-lan Chern National Taiwan Normal University; **Cheongsook Chin** English Campus Institute, Inje University; **Yang Hyun** Jung-Ang Girls' High School; **Li Junhe** Beijing No.4 High School; **Tim Knight** Gakushuin Women's College; **Ahmed M. Motala** University of Sharjah; **Gleides Ander Nonato** Colégio Arnaldo and Centro Universitário Newton Paiva; **Ethel Ogane** Tamagawa University; **Seung Ku Park** Sunmoon University; **Shu-chien, Sophia, Pan** College of Liberal Education, Shu-Te University; **Marlene Tavares de Allmeida** Wordshop Escola de Linguas; **Naowarat Tongkam** Silpakorn University; **Nobuo Tsuda** Konan University; **Hasan Hüseyin Zeyrek** Istanbul Kültür University Faculty of Economics and Administrative Sciences

Reviewers of the first edition

Penny Allan Languages Institute, Mount Royal College; **Jeremy Bishop** Ehwa Women's University; **William E. Brazda** Long Beach City College; **Michelle Buuck** Centennial College; **Chih-min Chou** National Chengchi University; **Karen Cronin** Shinjuku, Tokyo; **Marta O. Dmytrenko-Ahrabian** Wayne State University, English Language Institute; **James Goddard** Kwansei University; **Ann-Marie Hadzima** National Taiwan University; **Diane Hawley Nagatomo** Ochanomizu University; **Carolyn Ho** North Harris College; **Feng-Sheng Hung** National Kaohsiung First University of Science and Technology; **Yuko Iwata** Tokai University; **Johanna E. Katchen** National Tsing Hua University, Department of Foreign Languages; **Peter Kipp** Ehwa Women's University; **Julie Manning** Ritsumeikan Uji High School; **Gloria McPherson** English Language Institute, Seneca College; **Mary E. Meloy Lara** John F. Kennedy Primary School; **Young-in Moon** English Language and Literature Department, The University of Seoul; **Junil Oh** Pukyong National University; **Serdar Ozturk** Terraki Vakfı Okullarj; **Diana Pelyk** Ritsumeikan Asia Pacific University; **Stephen Russell** Meiji Gakuin University; **Consuelo Sañudo** Subsecretaria de Servicios Educativos para el Distrito Federal; **Robin Strickler** Kansai Gaidai University; **Liu Su-Fen** Mingchi Institute of Technology; **Cynthia Cheng-Fang** Tsui National Chengchi University; **Beatrice Vanni** University of Bahcesehir; **Kerry Vrabel** LaGuardia Community College; **Aysen Yurdakul** Buyuk Kolej

Contents

Unit	Chapter	Reading Skill	Vocabulary Skill	Real Life Skill
1 Travel *Page 11*	*Selling India's Rainy Season* Magazine Article	Predicting	The Prefix *off-*	Planning a Trip Online
	Avoiding Cultural Taboos Webpage	Scanning	Organizing Vocabulary	
2 Fashion *Page 23*	*Fashionable Decisions* Magazine Article	Skimming for the Main Idea	The Root Word *dic/dict*	Understanding Clothing Sizes
	Tom Ford—Master Designer Biography	Recognizing Sequence Markers	The Use of *Dress*	
3 Disappearing Animals *Page 35*	*Endangered Species* Encyclopedia Article	Identifying Meaning from Context	The Prefixes *ex-, en-,* and *em-*	Dictionary Usage: Choosing the Right Word
	Bring Back the Woolly Mammoth? Magazine Article	Indentifying Main Ideas within Paragraphs	The Suffix *-ize*	
Review 1 *Page 47*	**Fluency Strategy:** DRTA; *Ecotourism* Reference Article **Fluency Practice: 1.** *Modern Fashion Trends* Webpage; **2.** *Endangered Animal Success Stories* Newspaper Article			
4 Big Money *Page 57*	*What Does a Million Dollars Buy?* Reference Article	Identifying Cause and Effect	The Prefixes *in-, im-, il-,* and *ir-*	Understanding Money and Banking Terms
	Lottery Winners—Rich, but Happy? Magazine Article	Previewing	Noun and Adjective Suffixes *-ent* and *-ant*	
5 Cultural Events *Page 69*	*Wedding Customs* Encyclopedia Article	Skimming for the Main Idea	Word Families	Accepting and Declining Invitations
	That Unique Japanese Holiday Called . . . Christmas! Reference Article	Predicting	Homophones	
6 It's a Mystery *Page 81*	*Mystery Tours* Travel Brochure	Identifying Fact versus Theory	The Root Word *spec* + Prefixes	Researching Mysteries Online
	Is "Spontaneous Human Combustion" Possible? Reference Article	Identifying Meaning from Context	Collocations	
Review 2 *Page 93*	**Fluency Strategy:** KWL; *America's Biggest Lottery Winner* Magazine Article **Fluency Practice: 3.** *Married in a Kimono, Happy in Switzerland* Webpage; **4.** *The Truth Behind* The Da Vinci Code Magazine Article			

Unit	Chapter	Reading Skill	Vocabulary Skill	Real Life Skill
7 **Health** *Page 103*	*Successful Dieting* Online Message Board	Scanning	Creating Word Webs	Recognizing Common Medical Abbreviations
	Survival at the South Pole Newspaper Article	Predicting	The Prefixes *over-* and *under-*	
8 **Space and Flight** *Page 115*	*Human Adaptation to Space* Encyclopedia Article	Identifying Main and Supporting Ideas	The Prefixes *dis-* and *de-*	Dictionary Usage: Identifying Parts of Speech
	Pioneers of Flight Webpage	Making Inferences	Idioms with *Time*: Inferring Meaning from Context	
9 **The Changing Family** *Page 127*	*Is an Only Child a Lonely Child?* Advice Column	Recognizing Facts	Compound Nouns	Describing Family Relationships
	Changing Roles: Stay-at-Home Dads Webpage	Previewing	The Root Words *pater, mater,* and *juv*	
Review 3 *Page 139*	**Fluency Strategy:** SQ3R; *The Dangers of Dieting* Magazine Article **Fluency Practice:** 5. *Space Travel and Science Fiction* Book Extract; 6. *Single-Parent Families: Changing Views* Reference Article			
10 **Education** *Page 149*	*Homeschooling— A Better Way to Learn?* Reference Article	Arguing For and Against a Topic	The Root Word *ven/vent*	Identifying Common Academic Abbreviations
	Suggestopedia Encyclopedia Article	Identifying Meaning from Context	The Suffixes *-ible* and *-able*	
11 **The Mystery of Memory** *Page 161*	*How Good Is Your Memory?* Magazine Article	Skimming for the Main Idea	The Root Word *fic/fice*	Using Spelling Rules
	Words to Remember Reference Article	Scanning	Vocabulary-Recall Strategies	
12 **Art and Literature** *Page 173*	*Zorro: A Review* Book Review	Skimming for Opinions and Attitudes	Compound Adjectives	Reading Online Movie Reviews
	From Comic Books to Graphic Novels Magazine Article	Identifying Main and Supporting Ideas	Antonyms	
Review 4 *Page 185*	**Fluency Strategy:** Thinking *ACTIVEly* While Reading; *Korean Americans at GBS High School* Magazine Article **Fluency Practice:** 7. *You Can Be a World Memory Champion!* Webpage; 8. *Manga, Manhwa, and Manhua* Reference Article			

Vocabulary Learning Tips

Learning new vocabulary is an important part of learning to be a good reader. Remember that the letter **C** in **ACTIVE Skills for Reading** reminds us to cultivate vocabulary.

1 Decide if the word is worth learning now

As you read you will find many words you do not know. You will slow your reading fluency if you stop at every new word. For example, you should stop to find out the meaning of a new word if:
   a. you read the same word many times.
   b. the word appears in the heading of a passage, or in the topic sentence of a paragraph—the sentence that gives the main idea of the paragraph.

2 Record information about new words you decide to learn

Keep a vocabulary notebook in which you write words you want to remember. Complete the following information for words that you think are important to learn:

New word	collect
Translation	收集
Part of speech	verb
Sentence where found	Jamie Oliver collected more than 270,000 signatures from people.
My own sentence	My brother collects stamps.

3 Learn words from the same family

For many important words in English that you will want to learn, the word is part of a word family. As you learn new words, learn words in the family from other parts of speech (nouns, verbs, adjectives, adverbs, etc.).

Noun	happiness
Verb	
Adjective	happy
Adverb	happily

4 Learn words that go with the key word you are learning

When we learn new words, it is important to learn what other words are frequently used with them. These are called collocations. Here is an example from a student's notebook.

take		long		
go on	a	two-week	vacation	next week
need		short		in Italy
have		summer		with my family
		school		by myself

5 *Create a word web*

A word web is a picture that helps you connect words together and helps you increase your vocabulary. Here is a word web for the word "frightened":

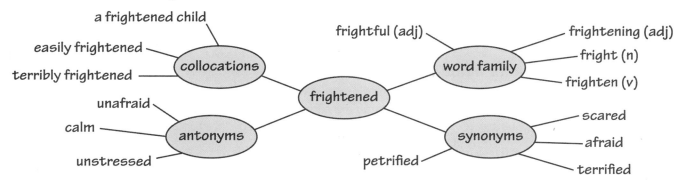

6 *Memorize common prefixes, roots, and suffixes*

Many English words can be divided into different parts. We call these parts *prefixes*, *roots*, and *suffixes*. A *prefix* comes at the beginning of a word, a *suffix* comes at the end of a word, and the *root* is the main part of the word. In your vocabulary notebook, make a list of prefixes and suffixes as you come across them. On pages 174–175 there is a list of prefixes and suffixes in this book. For example, look at the word "unhappily."

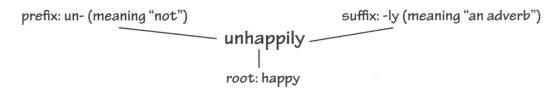

7 *Regularly review your vocabulary notebook*

You should review the words in your vocabulary notebook very often. The more often you review your list of new words, the sooner you will be able to recognize the words when you see them during reading. Set up a schedule to go over the words you are learning.

8 *Make vocabulary flash cards*

Flash cards are easy to make, and you can carry them everywhere with you. You can use them to study while you are waiting for the bus, walking to school or work, or eating a meal. You can use the flash cards with your friends to quiz each other. Here is an example of a flash card:

Front

Back

Tips for Fluent Reading

Find time to read every day.

Find the best time of day for you to read. Try to read when you are not tired. By reading every day, even for a short period, you will become a more fluent reader.

Look for a good place to read.

It is easier to read and study if you are comfortable. Make sure that there is good lighting in your reading area and that you are sitting in a comfortable chair. To make it easier to concentrate, try to read in a place where you won't be interrupted.

Use clues in the text to make predictions.

Fluent readers make predictions before and as they read. Use the title, subtitle, pictures, and captions to ask yourself questions about what you are going to read. Find answers to the questions when you read. After reading, think about what you have learned and decide what you need to read next to continue learning.

Establish goals before you read.

Before you read a text, think about the purpose of your reading. For example, do you just want to get a general idea of the passage? Or do you need to find specific information? Thinking about what you want to get from the reading will help you decide what reading skills you need to use.

Notice how your eyes and head are moving.

Good readers use their eyes, and not their heads, when they read. Moving your head back and forth when reading will make you tired. Practice avoiding head movements by placing your elbows on the table and resting your head in your hands. Do you feel movement as you read? If you do, hold your head still as you read. Also, try not to move your eyes back over a text. You should reread part of a text only when you have a specific purpose for rereading, for example, to make a connection between what you read previously and what you are reading now.

Try not to translate.

Translation slows down your reading. Instead of translating new words into your first language, first try to guess the meaning. Use the context (the other words around the new word) and word parts (prefixes, suffixes, and word roots) to help you guess the meaning.

Read in phrases rather than word by word.

Don't point at each word while you read. Practice reading in phrases—groups of words that go together.

Engage your imagination.

Good readers visualize what they are reading. They create a movie in their head of the story they are reading. As you read, try sharing with a partner the kinds of pictures that you create in your mind.

Avoid subvocalization.

Subvocalization means quietly saying the words as you read. You might be whispering the words or just silently saying them in your mind. Your eyes and brain can read much faster than you can speak. If you subvocalize, you can only read as fast as you can say the words. As you read, place your finger on your lips or your throat. Do you feel movement? If so, you are subvocalizing. Practice reading without moving your lips.

Don't worry about understanding every word.

Sometimes, as readers, we think we must understand the meaning of everything that we read. It isn't always necessary to understand every word in a passage in order to understand the meaning of the passage as a whole. Instead of interrupting your reading to find the meaning of a new word, circle the word and come back to it after you have finished reading.

Enjoy your reading.

Your enjoyment of reading will develop over time. Perhaps today you do not like to read in English, but as you read more, you should see a change in your attitude. The more you read in English, the easier it will become. You will find yourself looking forward to reading.

Read as much as you can.

The best tip to follow to become a more fluent reader is to read whenever and wherever you can. Good readers read a lot. They read many different kinds of material: newspapers, magazines, textbooks, websites, and graded readers. To practice this, keep a reading journal. Every day, make a list of the kinds of things you read during the day and how long you read each for. If you want to become a more fluent reader, read more!

Are You an ACTIVE Reader?

Before you use this book to develop your reading skills, think about your reading habits, and your strengths and weaknesses when reading in English. Check the statements that are true for you.

		Start of course	End of course
1	I read something in English every day.	☐	☐
2	I try to read where I'm comfortable and won't be interrupted.	☐	☐
3	I make predictions about what I'm going to read before I start reading.	☐	☐
4	I think about my purpose of reading before I start reading.	☐	☐
5	I keep my head still, and move only my eyes, when I read.	☐	☐
6	I try not to translate words from English to my first language.	☐	☐
7	I read in phrases rather than word by word.	☐	☐
8	I try to picture in my mind what I'm reading.	☐	☐
9	I read silently, without moving my lips.	☐	☐
10	I try to understand the meaning of the passage, and try not to worry about understanding the meaning of every word.	☐	☐
11	I usually enjoy reading in English.	☐	☐
12	I try to read as much as I can, especially outside class.	☐	☐

Follow the tips on pages 8–9. These will help you become a more active reader. At the end of the course, answer this quiz again to see if you have become a more fluent, active reader.

Cultural and Exotic Vacations, Inc.

Cultural and Exotic Vacations has assembled an impressive array of vacations to far-off locales that offer unique cultural experiences as well as breathtaking sightseeing opportunities. Each of our tours has been created by an expert traveler who has already experienced the tour. We make sure to include plenty of one-of-a-kind participatory experiences to make your vacation unforgettable.

The Two Capitals of Russia

Discover Moscow and St. Petersburg. Included is an unforgettable night at the ballet in Moscow and a tour of the famous Hermitage museum.

Adventure Down Under

See the unique people, landscape, and wildlife of Australia. The tour includes diving on the Great Barrier Reef and a four-wheel drive Outback tour.

Tanzania Safari

Experience the wonders of African wildlife, courtesy of our experienced guides. Enjoy walking tours and bird watching with local villagers.

Shopping Tour of Hong Kong

Enjoy a customized shopping tour of the best shopping in this bustling city. You'll stop for an elegant "tea time" in the Peninsula Hotel lobby.

Getting Ready

Discuss the following questions with a partner.

1 Which of the vacation packages above interests you the most? Why?
2 Can you think of a difference between the cultures of the places mentioned above and your own?
3 What other cultural or exotic vacations would you like to experience?
4 How should we prepare before visiting a completely different culture?

Unit 1   *Chapter 1: Selling India's Rainy Season*

Before You Read:
Weather and Vacations

Discuss the following questions with a partner.

1 What kind of weather do you like the best when on vacation?
2 Have you ever been on vacation in unpleasant weather?
3 Where would you like to go on vacation for the following types of weather?

Type of weather	Destination
snowy	_____
rainy	_____
very hot	_____
rather cool and breezy	_____

Reading Skill:
Predicting

Before reading, good readers think about what they are going to read. While reading, good readers think about what comes next. This helps them better understand what comes next.

A Read the title of the article and answer the following questions.

1 Who is probably interested in "selling India's rainy season"?
  a. Indian companies that sell water to neighboring countries
  b. tour operators who want to convince tourists to visit India during the rainy season
  c. Indian weather scientists who are researching ways of preventing the rainy season
2 Which Indian industry does the rainy season probably hurt the most?
  a. the agricultural industry
  b. the fishing industry
  c. the tourism industry
3 What group of people are interested in coming to India during the rainy season?
  a. wealthy people who can afford an expensive vacation
  b. people from dry countries
  c. water control engineers

B Skim the article to see if your answers were correct.

C Read the article again, then answer the questions that follow.

Selling India's Rainy Season

TRAVEL

In the spring, the heat **intensifies** over the northern Indian plains, pulling in **humid** air from the Arabian Gulf to the southwest. The first storms begin with dramatic displays of thunder and lightning, and by July the rains sweep across the entire country. The rainy season, which lasts until October, brings cooler temperatures, new life to the dry, brown fields, and often floods in the wettest areas.

This is the monsoon,[1] traditionally a joyful and very important time for Indian agricultural workers. It has been less happy for those who work in the tourist trade, because the number of visitors in this season tends to drop by half. For the last few years, however, there has been a movement to increase tourism, both foreign and domestic, during this normally slow time of the year. The agreed-upon goal is to bring more tourists to selected parts of the country. According to a report issued by an Indian industry group, appropriate destinations for the monsoon season must remain **accessible** by road during the wettest months and have a countryside that looks its best during the rains.

Tourist agencies in various states have responded to the challenge. Goa, the former Portuguese **colony** near Mumbai, and Kerala in the extreme south have begun offering "monsoon packages." They say there are many reasons in addition to the reduced, **off-season** prices to visit their states during this time of the year. One is to see the lush,[2] green landscapes. "Goa has beautiful islands, waterfalls, lakes, dams, and wildlife **sanctuaries** that can be enjoyed during the monsoons," says Elvis Gomes, previous director of the tourism department in the state. Other attractions are the many colorful festivals. For example, Sri Jagannath Yatra, a festival held around the country at the beginning of the monsoon, features a colorful **procession**. A third is simply the joy of the season. As one Kerala promoter says, "The splashing waters make the monsoon the favorite season in India. You can feel the magic. The washed streets and fresh leaves seem to smile with you."

Resorts in the rain-soaked areas have added special **facilities** designed to attract monsoon visitors. For example, some have built "water

parks," areas with a series of connected pools,
50 water slides, and fountains which people can
splash around in, and open-air discos where
people can dance when it pours. Some hotels
have also constructed private patios next to
their guest rooms so that their guests can
55 shower naturally in the rain.

The idea of enjoying a rainy holiday seems
strange to many, but it has definite **allure** for
Arab tourists from the dry Persian Gulf coast.
To these visitors, rain is a very unusual event,
60 and a wet vacation sounds exotic and delightful.
Indian tour operators have taken notice and have
started organizing special monsoon tours for Gulf

visitors. Many of these guests come
with their families and like to stay at large
65 resorts where they can spend time together at
the water parks or just sitting around a pool.
Most visitors at the resort stay inside during wet
weather, but these guests appear to prefer to be
outdoors, even (or especially) when it rains. As
70 fathers and their children in bathing suits swim
or play in the rain, the ladies of the family, fully
clothed but without umbrellas, sit and watch nearby.
All are soaking wet and having a great time. As a
recent visitor explained, "If we had wanted to be
75 in air conditioning, we could have just stayed in
Kuwait."

¹**monsoon** a season of heavy rainstorms, especially in India and Southeast Asia
²**lush** with thick, heavy growth

Reading Comprehension:
Check Your
Understanding

A The statements below are about the reading. Choose the correct answer
to complete each one.

1 The writer's point of view seems to indicate that he or she _____.
   a. works for the Indian government
   b. doesn't believe the tourist trade can grow in the rainy season
   c. wishes to describe the situation in a balanced way
2 The rainy season in India is _____ months long.
   a. three   b. four   c. five
3 The monsoon season is a traditionally happy one for Indian _____.
   a. tourists   b. agricultural workers   c. construction workers
4 During the rainy season, tourism in India tends to _____.
   a. increase by 50%   b. drop by half   c. stay about the same
5 Compared to other times of the year, visiting India in the rainy season is _____.
   a. less expensive   b. more expensive   c. equally expensive

B Decide whether the following statements about the reading are true (T), false (F), or if the information is not given (NG). If you check (✔) false, correct the statement to make it true.

	T	F	NG
1 During the rainy season, there are often floods in the driest areas of India.			
2 India wants to increase tourism from foreign countries and within India.			
3 One Indian festival involves throwing colored powder.			
4 Some people dance and others take showers in the rain.			
5 The Persian Gulf coast is a particularly wet area.			

C Critical Thinking

Discuss these questions with a partner.
1 Would you like to take a vacation in India during the rainy season?
2 Why do Elvis Gomes and the Kerala promoter mentioned in the reading speak so highly of the rainy season in India?
3 This article describes quite a few positive points of a rainy season vacation in India. What might be some of the negative points?

Vocabulary Comprehension: Odd Word Out

A For each group, circle the word that does not belong. The words in *italics* are vocabulary items from the reading.

1 available	obtainable	*accessible*	impossible
2 repulsion	interest	*allure*	attraction
3 *colony*	enemy	outpost	territory
4 equipment	fixtures	foodstuffs	*facilities*
5 damp	*humid*	muggy	brisk
6 *intensify*	modify	strengthen	build up
7 off-peak	slow period	*off-season*	offspring
8 parade	*procession*	marchers	party
9 *sanctuary*	invasion	refuge	preserve

B Complete the sentences using the words in *italics* from A. Be sure to use the correct form of the word.

1 I much prefer dry weather, although _____ weather is quite good for most plants.
2 That island is a _____ for birds. They can live there undisturbed by people.
3 That top secret information is only _____ to the president and his closest advisors.

4 Tattoos have a great _____ for young people. They all think they're cool and want to get one.

5 There were nearly 10,000 people walking through the streets in costumes in the holiday _____.

6 The doctor told me to take two pills if the pain _____.

7 Hotel rates are always significantly lower during the _____.

8 Before 1776, the United States was a _____ of Great Britain.

9 Modern prisons have more educational _____ than older ones, for example libraries, classrooms, and computers.

Vocabulary Skill:

The Prefix *off-*

In this chapter, you learned the noun "off-season" meaning "a time of reduced activity." This word is formed by adding the prefix "off-" to the noun "season." The prefix "off-" can mean "away from," "out of," or "not on."

A What do you think the following words mean? Match each word with a definition on the right.

1 offbeat   _____   a. informal and without planning
2 offhand   _____   b. a highway exit
3 off-key   _____   c. not on the correct musical note
4 off-kilter   _____   d. in a place where there are no streets
5 off-line   _____   e. disconnected from a system,
6 off-limits   e.g., the Internet
7 off-road   _____   f. not to be entered or used
8 off-ramp   _____   g. unusual
9 offshore   _____   h. not in perfect balance
10 offscreen   _____   i. not shown in movies or on TV; away
                           from the camera
                   _____   j. away from land; out in the ocean

B Now use the words in A to complete these sentences. Check your answers with a partner.

1 My brother has taken a lot of singing lessons, but he still sings _____.

2 The army base is _____ to everyone except military personnel.

3 Although he seems arrogant in his movies, that star is very shy and polite _____.

4 Having exhausted supplies on land, many companies now drill for oil _____.

5 Before giving his speech, the president answered a few _____ questions.

6 No matter how many times I straighten it, that picture on the wall ends up _____.

7 I love searching furniture shops for unique pieces with _____ designs.

8 I need to get into the office network, but my computer is still _____.

9 Don't miss the _____, or we'll need to drive 20 kilometers to the next one.

10 In order to drive _____ you need to have a four-wheel-drive vehicle.

Chapter 2: Avoiding Cultural Taboos

A How well do you know your own culture? Write a rule for correct cultural behavior in each of the following areas.

dining _____

introducing yourself in a business setting

_____

wearing certain colors of clothes _____

being punctual _____

physical contact _____

smoking _____

B Compare your answers with a partner. Then discuss what happens when someone breaks each of the rules you wrote.

Before You Read:
Cultural Awareness

A Under which subtitle would you expect to find the following topics? Match the topics with the subtitles.

1 kissing

2 covering your shoulders

3 pointing at someone

4 wrapping paper

5 asking too many questions

6 clocks and fans

_____ **a.** Speech and gestures

_____ **b.** Religious customs

_____ **c.** Sensitive topics

_____ **d.** Displaying affection

_____ **e.** Choosing gifts

_____ **f.** Opening gifts

B Now scan the subtitled sections to see if you were correct.

C Read the passage, then answer the questions that follow.

Reading Skill:
Scanning

When we want to find certain information in a text, we don't actually read the text, we "scan" it. We move our eyes very quickly across the page to look for the information we need, sometimes using subtitles, numbers, or other key words to help us. Scanning can help you save time looking for information in a text.

Avoiding Cultural Taboos

Thanks to the speed and convenience of modern travel, destinations that used to take a long time to travel to can now be reached quickly and easily. Even though jet flights
5 make **far-off locales** seem close, they may still be different from your home country in various important ways. Therefore, it is important to **adapt** your behavior so that you don't insult or offend the local people. Here
10 are some tips that will make communication easier, and your trip more enjoyable.

1 Speech and gestures

Never raise your voice in order to make yourself understood. If you do not know the word for something in the local language, or cannot make yourself understood verbally, try drawing a picture
15 or pointing to an object. Remember, though, that pointing directly at a person can be highly offensive in some cultures. If you have to point something out, do so by gesturing towards the object with the palm of your hand flat, facing upward, and your fingers outstretched. Before you travel, try learning some basic words or phrases of the local language. Most useful are those that express **gratitude** and politeness, such as words for *please*, *thank you*, and *may I*, as well as basic greetings.

20 2 Religious customs

Consider the main religion of the country you plan to visit and read about any taboos related to clothing, especially if you plan to visit places that are considered **sacred**. As a precaution, bring **conservative** clothes, such as shirts or T-shirts that cover your shoulders, and long trousers.

3 Sensitive topics

25 Avoid topics of conversation that you think may be sensitive. If a topic is sensitive in your own culture, it will more than likely be the same in other cultures. Feel free to show interest in the history and customs of the place you are visiting, but don't ask too many questions about why things are done a certain way; you may offend the local people.

4 Displaying affection

30 Keep in mind that, in many cultures, displaying **affection** in public is considered taboo. Kissing on the street or in public places is unacceptable behavior and should be avoided. If you are unsure of how to behave, watch the local people and copy them—if they don't behave in a certain way, you probably shouldn't either.

5 Choosing gifts

If you are traveling on business, or plan to stay with a host family, and you wish to take a gift, do some research. The idea of the perfect gift varies greatly from country to country, and one of the easiest ways to offend somebody is to give the wrong gift. In China, it is taboo to give clocks and fans. The Chinese word for "fan" has a similar sound to the word for "separation," while the sound for "clock" is similar to that of "death." In Japan, gifts should never be given in sets of four, as the sound of the word "four" in Japanese is similar to the sound of the word meaning "death."

6 Opening gifts

The opening of gifts is also treated very differently around the world. In many Western countries, do not be surprised if your hosts immediately tear the wrapping paper from a gift in great excitement. They will then tell you how wonderful the gift is, even if they do not like it! In most Asian countries, it is considered impolite to open gifts in front of the gift-giver for fear of offending the person.

Wherever you go in the world, always be **tolerant** of the local customs. Avoid being **critical**; try instead to show respect for the values of the country you are in, even if you do not necessarily agree with them.

A For each question or statement, choose the best answer.

Reading Comprehension: Check Your Understanding

1 The author of the reading passage has most likely _____.
   a. traveled a lot   **b.** taught at a university   **c.** written several books
2 According to the reading, which articles of clothing should you plan to travel with?
   a. a T-shirt and shorts   **b.** a jacket and hat   **c.** pants and a long-sleeved shirt
3 If a topic isn't appropriate to talk about in your country, it probably _____ okay to talk about in another country.
   a. might be   **b.** should be   **c.** isn't
4 According to the reading, _____ is not appropriate behavior in many countries.
   a. kissing in public   **b.** expressing gratitude   **c.** giving presents
5 According to the reading, the best gift to give someone from China is _____.
   a. a fan   **b.** a clock   **c.** neither a nor b

B The statements below are about the reading. Complete each one using the correct word or phrase.

1 It's useful to learn the words for *please*, *thank you*, *may I*, as well as
   _____.
2 When you're unsure about how to behave, watch the _____.
3 The Chinese word for *clock* and the Japanese word for *four* both have the same sound as the word meaning _____.
4 In Asian countries it is considered impolite to open gifts _____ the giver of the gift.
5 While in another country, if a local person can't understand something you are saying, try _____ or pointing to the object.

C Critical Thinking

Discuss these questions with a partner.

1 Which topic that the author covered do you think is the most important? Why?

2 What other topic could be included in this reading passage?

Vocabulary Comprehension:
Word Definitions

A Look at the list of words and phrases from the reading. Match each with a definition on the right.

1 far-off   a. place

2 locale   b. patient; able to bear annoyance well

3 adapt   c. deserving of religious respect

4 gratitude   d. a feeling of liking or love

5 sacred   e. not modern; cautious

6 conservative   f. thankfulness

7 affection   g. pointing out what is wrong

8 tolerant   h. change to be more suitable

9 critical   i. distant

B Compete the sentences below using the vocabulary from A. Be sure to use the correct form of the word.

1 When Jamie moved into her own apartment, it took her a while to _____ to living alone.

2 Clara's father has some very _____ beliefs. For example, he thinks a woman shouldn't work after she gets married.

3 After receiving a gift in the United States, it's common to send a thank-you card to express one's _____.

4 That beach community has become a favorite _____ for retired people to live in.

5 Jack's parents are too _____ of their son's bad behavior. They let him do whatever he likes.

6 Hiromi has a great deal of _____ for her grandfather and visits him at least once a week.

7 I've been to many neighboring countries, but I've never traveled to any really _____ places.

8 Kristin and Marcus disagree a lot, and they are very _____ of each other's opinions.

9 Churches, mosques, and temples are _____ places for religious activities.

A One way to organize words is to group them by part of speech.
Write the part of speech (noun (n) or adjective (a)) for each word below.

Word	Part of speech		Word	Part of speech
facilities	_____		aggressive	_____
fundamental	_____		sacred	_____
acceptable	_____		tolerant	_____
offensive	_____		locale	_____
grateful	_____		forbidden	_____
critical	_____		affectionate	_____
allure	_____		confident	_____
insulting	_____			

B Another way to organize these words is to use a more descriptive category—for example, words that are positive, negative, or neutral. Put the adjectives from A into one or all of the categories below.

Positive	Negative	Neutral
tolerant	critical	locale

C Vocabulary can also be grouped by topic. What are some topics that you can use to organize the adjectives above? Think of a topic, and then list the adjectives from A that relate to it in the chart below. Share your ideas with a partner.

Topic	Adjectives

One helpful way to remember new words is to group them into meaningful categories, for example, by part of speech or topic. Organizing your vocabulary can also help you to relate new vocabulary to other words you know.

Real Life Skill:
Planning a Trip Online

While travel agents are tremendously helpful, particularly for complex international journeys, millions of independent-minded travelers are using the Internet to learn about destinations, find last-minute bargains, and locate hotels. The Internet puts the tools for trip planning into the hands of average computer users, enabling them to plan their own trips at their own convenience.

A Think of a vacation destination you would like to visit and complete the chart.

Destination	Hawaii	
Transportation	airplane	
Accommodation	luxury resort	
Activities	surfing, cycling, swimming	
Other information	made up of 18 islands	

B Next you will search for transportation, accommodations, three activities, and other information for your destination on the Internet. Perform an Internet search for each and complete the chart.

	Search words	Company	Price
Transportation			
Accommodation			
Activity 1			
Activity 2			
Activity 3			
Other information			

C Share the information you found with a group of classmates. Find out whose trip plan is the most popular with the group.

What Do You Think?

1 What are some of the ways that the tourist trade is promoted in your country?
2 What are some of the ways that too much tourism can impact a vacation locale?
3 Imagine that you and your partner are planning a trip to a country whose culture is very different from yours. List some of the ways you would need to adapt your behavior while visiting.

Getting Ready

Discuss the following questions with a partner.

1 Look at the photos above. Describe what the people in each photo are wearing. Use the following vocabulary to help you:

> miniskirt   platform shoes   high heels   go-go boots   bow tie

2 Describe the clothes you are wearing at the moment. What do your clothes tell people about you?

3 How do men's and women's fashions differ?

4 Do you consider yourself to be a fashion-conscious person? Explain your answer.

Before You Read:

How Trendy Are You?

A Discuss the following questions with a partner.

1 What do you understand by the word *fashionable*? Name a person who you think is fashionable.
2 What is the most fashionable article of clothing you own?
3 What fashions are "in style" right now?

B What kinds of clothes were popular in these decades? With a partner, try to think of at least one example for each.

The 1950s _____

The 1960s _____

The 1970s _____

The 1980s _____

The 1990s _____

Reading Skill:

Skimming for the Main Idea

Skimming is one way to look for the main ideas in a reading. When we skim, we read over parts of the text very quickly. We don't need to read every word or look up words we don't understand; we just need to get a general idea of what something is about.

A Skim the passage quickly. Read only the title, the first and last paragraphs, and the first sentence of the other paragraphs. Don't worry about words you don't know. Then, complete the sentence.

This passage is mainly about _____.
a. clothing makers who have created some of the world's most important fashions
b. why fashion styles from the 1960s, '70s, '80s, and '90s are still popular today
c. what fashion is and what fashions have been influential in recent decades

B Compare your answer with a partner. Explain why you chose it, including any evidence you found when skimming the passage.

C Read through the passage again, then answer the questions that follow.

FASHIONABLE DECISIONS

Fashion trends aren't only **dictated** by a few well-known clothing designers. Some people use their clothes to **make a statement** about individual style, beliefs, musical tastes, or cultural identity. Additionally, celebrities have always had a very direct influence on what is **trendy** or in fashion. Just look around, and you'll see young people trying to create the same "look" as the movie stars, pop musicians, or other famous people that they **idolize**. Looking back at changes in clothing styles over past **decades**, it seems that fashion trends tend to occur in cycles.

THE 1950s

White T-shirts, patent leather[1] shoes, and slicked-back hair were **essential** for young men in the '50s. Popular fashions for young women were poodle skirts and calf-length slacks called "pedal-pushers." Many young men **imitated** the fashion of Elvis Presley and movie star James Dean. Young women looked to movie stars such as Audrey Hepburn.

THE 1960s

This decade saw many changes in the way young people dressed. As the decade continued, young people grew their hair longer, and a much more comfortable, casual look became popular. Both men and women wore tight jeans that widened from the knee down, often personalized with patches or drawings. T-shirts were still popular with men, but now with new designs and slogans. For women, loose-fitting cotton blouses, flowery dresses, and fashion designer Mary Quant's invention, the miniskirt, were very popular. Both men and women took their fashion **cues** from the many rock bands and singers that exploded on the scene. U.S. first lady Jacqueline Kennedy also greatly influenced women's fashion.

THE 1970s

In the 1970s, both men and women wore bell-bottom pants, wide lapels,[2] and platform shoes. This was the disco period, and shirts made of **synthetic** materials had brilliant colors and sometimes dizzying patterns. By the end of the decade, the punk fashion movement with its spiky hair, torn clothes, and Dr. Martens boots had begun. Fashion icons of the decade included John Travolta, Farah Fawcett, and David Bowie.

THE 1980s

Although the punk influence continued, many young men got much neater and more conservative in designer jeans and polo shirts. Young women wore dresses and jackets with big shoulder pads. A new cultural emphasis on exercise led to new casual wear, such as brilliantly colored sweatsuits and running suits of new synthetic materials. For women, Princess Diana was very influential, as were the television series *Dynasty* and *Dallas* for both women and men.

THE 1990s

40   Perhaps partly as a reaction to the formal, businesslike '80s, casual style was extremely popular in the 1990s. Companies permitted, and even encouraged, a "business casual" look. Both women and men wore loose-fitting trousers. Asian influences were seen in the popularity of cheongsam dresses and the new wave of inexpensive Asian-made accessories. In addition, the "retro" look—combining styles of earlier decades—became quite popular. Gwen Stefani,

45   Jennifer Aniston, boy bands such as Backstreet Boys, and fashion designers Abercrombie & Fitch, Donna Karan, Tommy Hilfiger, Calvin Klein and Ralph Lauren were looked to for fashion leadership.

TODAY'S FASHION

Although we're too close to post-2000 fashion to really see it clearly, a few trends can be
50   perceived. The latest technology, such as mobile phone earpieces and MP3 players, has become part of a modern look. Midriffs have never been more popular, along with low-rise jeans, tattoos, and body piercing. The baggy, oversized clothes of the "gangsta" look remain popular with many young people. Britney Spears, Anna Kournikova, Justin Timberlake, and David Beckham have all been at the forefront of fashion trends.

55   The long and interesting history of fashion has provided us with many interesting choices. Perhaps the clothes you are wearing right now were inspired by celebrities, musicians, or cultural movements. In each decade there seems to be a change in style to allow us to make a statement about our taste and identity.

---

¹**patent leather** leather with a shiny finish on it
²**lapels** the two pieces of cloth on the front of a coat or jacket that attach to the collar

---

Reading Comprehension:
Check Your Understanding

A Complete the sentences about the reading.

1   The clothes a person chooses to wear can tell others about his or her _____ _____.

2   In the 1950s, fashion role models for young men included _____ _____.

3   In which decade did the punk movement begin? _____ _____.

4   According to the article, which two television series had a powerful influence on fashion? _____.

5   The "retro" look can be described as _____ _____.

B Match the fashion items with the decade in which they were popular.

1	designer jeans, polo shirts, shoulder pads _____	**a.** 1950s
2	tight jeans, flowery blouses, miniskirts _____	**b.** 1960s
3	poodle skirts, pedal pushers _____	**c.** 1970s
4	loose-fitting trousers, Asian-made accessories _____	**d.** 1980s
5	bell-bottom pants, wide lapels, platform shoes _____	**e.** 1990s

C Critical Thinking

Discuss these questions with a partner.
1 Why do you think fashions constantly change over time?
2 Do certain cities or countries seem to be leaders in fashion? If so, which ones?
3 What do you think the expression "a slave to fashion" means?

Vocabulary Comprehension:
Word Definitions

A Look at the vocabulary items below, from the reading. Write *noun, verb,* or *adjective* to describe each word's part of speech as it is used in the reading.

1 cue _____
2 decade _____
3 dictate _____
4 essential _____
5 idolize _____

6 imitate _____
7 make (a statement) _____
8 synthetic _____
9 trendy _____

B Look at the definitions below. Now match each word or phrase from A to its definition.

_____ **a.** to copy something or try to be like someone else
_____ **b.** to make your opinion about something known publicly
_____ **c.** to admire or respect
_____ **d.** absolutely necessary
_____ **e.** fashionable; in style

_____ **f.** a signal for someone else to follow
_____ **g.** man-made
_____ **h.** a period of ten years
_____ **i.** to tell, usually to order or command someone to do something

C Circle the word or phrase that best completes each statement.

1 People who are critical of war often make a statement by (protesting / keeping informed about) international conflicts.
2 It is essential that hospital facilities be (beautiful / clean).
3 People who idolize pop stars often try to (look like / criticize) them.
4 A (cheap / designer) suit would probably not be considered trendy by many people.
5 Synthetic fabrics include rayon, nylon, and (cotton / polyester).
6 In most countries, the (media / law) dictates what people can or can't do.

7　Movie directors often use cues to (signal actors / write a scene).

8　I try to imitate Mahatma Gandhi by being very (tolerant / unpredictable).

9　Two decades represent a period of (20 / 40) years.

Vocabulary Skill:

The Root Word *dic/dict*

In this chapter you read the verb "dictate," meaning "to tell" or "command." This word is made by combining the root word "dict," meaning "to say, tell, or speak," with the verb suffix "-ate." "Dict," sometimes also written "dic," is combined with other root words, prefixes, and suffixes to form many words in English.

A For each word, study the different parts. Then, write the part of speech and a simple definition. Use your dictionary to help you. Share your ideas with a partner.

	Word	Part of Speech	Definition
1	dictate	_____	_____
2	dictator	_____	_____
3	diction	_____	_____
4	dictionary	_____	_____
5	contradict	_____	_____
6	indicate	_____	_____
7	predict	_____	_____
8	verdict	_____	_____

B Complete each sentence using the words from A. Be sure to use the correct form of the word.

1　Can I borrow your _____ for a minute? I need to look up a word.

2　At the end of the court trial, the jury announced its _____. The prisoner was guilty.

3　In the far-off country of Midoria, the ruler is a _____ who forces everyone to wear green clothes every day.

4　It's warm today, so I _____ that it will be a nice day tomorrow, too.

5　Even if you don't speak someone's language, you can _____ your gratitude through body language and facial expressions.

6　At first, Caroline said she liked the movie, but later she _____ herself and said that she didn't like it very much.

7　At first it was hard to understand Spanish, but my teacher has such good _____ that I can now hear many of the sounds easily.

8　I enjoy my freedom and definitely don't like other people to _____ to me what I have to do.

Before You Read:
Fashion Designers

A Which of these famous fashion designers have you heard of? With a partner, circle the ones you both know.

> Calvin Klein   Yves Saint Laurent   Gucci
> Vera Wang   Tommy Hilfiger   Jean Paul Gaultier

B What kinds of clothes are the fashion designers above famous for? Do you have a favorite fashion designer?

Reading Skill:
Recognizing Sequence Markers

A Scan the reading for the sentences below to find the sequence marker that connects each pair of events from Tom Ford's life story. Write the sequence marker in the blank.

1 The revolution was over _____ Tom Ford started working . . .
2 _____ completing high school, he moved to New York . . .
3 Ford completed a program in interior design, but _____ decided that he was more interested in designing clothes.
4 _____ his first years at Gucci, the company was going through a very difficult period.

B In each sentence in A above, circle the event that occurred first. If the events happened at the same time, circle both events.

C Read the passage again, then answer the questions that follow.

> Sequence markers are words and phrases that signal the reader about the order of events. Expressions such as "then," "soon after that," "subsequently," as well as days, dates, and times can act as sequence markers. The past perfect tense can also signal the order of events.

Tom Ford—Master Designer

The **revolution** was over by the time Tom Ford started working in the fashion world. The **exclusive** fashion design houses such as Chanel, Yves Saint Laurent, and Christian Dior, which earned money by designing and making very expensive **custom** clothes,
5   had lost many of their wealthy customers. To stay in business, they started selling more reasonably priced ready-to-wear clothing along with a wide range of accessories, that is, related products such as shoes, bags, watches, make-up kits, and perfumes. All of these products needed to blend with the clothing and with
10 each other so that they made up a brand that everyone would recognize and want to buy. Though they did not use that name, each company needed a "master designer."

Born in Texas and growing up in Santa Fe, New Mexico, Ford had a diverse background in the arts. Soon after completing high school, he moved to New York, where he studied art history, trained as an actor, and
15 worked as a model. Following that, Ford completed a program in **interior** design, but subsequently decided that he was more interested in designing clothes than in decorating houses. He was hired by the firm Cathy Hardwick in 1986, where he began to work as a fashion designer. His talents stood out from the rest and soon he moved to Perry Ellis, where he became design director. Then in 1990 he made a **crucial** move by taking a position with the New York branch of Gucci, the famous design house based in Milan, Italy.

20 During his first years at Gucci, the company was going through a very difficult period. Its products were once considered highly desirable, and were worn by famous women such as Grace Kelly, Audrey Hepburn, and Jacqueline Kennedy. However, by the early nineties they had lost their **reputation** for quality. Other producers had started making cheap, widely available imitations of the brand, and the sales of Gucci's own products had dropped. Things were so bad at one point that Ford was almost fired. However, some people
25 at the company believed in his talent, and in 1994 they hired him to work in Milan as the creative director for the entire company. In this position Ford had artistic control over all of the company's products, as well as its advertising and the design of its stores. Under Ford's direction, Gucci's reputation for **cutting-edge** style soon returned, and the company began to recover. The style shows starting in 1994 were wildly successful. People loved the low-cut velvet pants, unbuttoned silk shirts, and shiny boots in metallic colors.
30 By 1999 Gucci, which had almost gone out of business, was worth over $4 billion.

When Gucci bought Yves Saint Laurent, Ford became creative director for that fashion house while continuing to design for Gucci. When asked how he would be able to keep the two styles apart, Ford said it wasn't a problem and offered a comparison. Yves Saint Laurent was like Catherine Deneuve, he said, while Gucci was more like Sophia Loren. Both are sexy and beautiful women, but with very different styles.

35 His first YSL collection, a big hit, was **distinctive**, all right—all of the clothes were in black and white.

Ford left Gucci and Yves Saint Laurent in 2004 to form his own company called simply "Tom Ford." Not long after, he was working together with cosmetics producer Estee Lauder to bring out new beauty products, and then developed and sold a perfume under his own name. His plans for the future? Ford says that someday he'd definitely like to make a film. He puts it this way: "That is the **ultimate** design project.
40 You don't just get to design what people wear, but you design the whole world and whether characters get to live or die. There is a permanence to film that fashion lacks."

Reading Comprehension: Check Your Understanding

A Choose the best answer for each question or statement below.

1 Why did the author most likely write this passage?
   a. to describe the career of Tom Ford
   b. to show why Tom Ford is the world's greatest fashion designer
   c. to explain why Tom Ford was constantly changing jobs

2 Why did the famous design houses need a "master designer"?
   a. to make custom clothes for their wealthy customers
   b. to start a revolution in the fashion world
   c. to blend a wide range of accessories with ready-to-wear clothing

3 The passage doesn't mention that Ford received any training in _____.
   a. acting   b. modeling   c. photography

4 In the 1990s, what company was Ford able to help recover from an unsuccessful period?
   a. Gucci   b. Yves Saint Laurent   c. Perry Ellis

5 In the future, Tom Ford hopes to _____.
   a. create a perfume   b. make a movie   c. write a book

B In which order did Tom Ford work as a designer with the following design houses? Number them 1–5 in the correct order.

   _____ Gucci
   _____ Tom Ford
   _____ Perry Ellis
   _____ Cathy Hardwick
   _____ Yves Saint Laurent

Tom Ford—Master Designer 31

C Critical Thinking

Discuss these questions with a partner.

1 Do you like to wear designer clothes? Why or why not?
2 If you could be a designer, what kinds of clothes would you like to design?

Vocabulary Comprehension:
Words in Context

A **The words in *italics* are vocabulary items from the reading. Read each question or statement and choose the correct answer. Compare your answers with a partner.**

1 It is *crucial* for fashion designers to have a good sense of _____.
  a. color **b.** humor

2 *Custom* clothes are special because they are specially made _____.
  a. for one person **b.** in a foreign country

3 *Cutting-edge* fashions are _____.
  a. the most modern **b.** the most shocking

4 That movie star has a *distinctive* look; her appearance is quite _____ other actresses.
  a. similar to **b.** different from

5 That vacation locale has several *exclusive* resorts; _____ are allowed to use their facilities.
  a. only certain people **b.** all visitors

6 I need to hire an *interior* designer to _____.
  a. design my back yard **b.** design my bathroom

7 Because of Timothy's *reputation* in business, most of his customers _____.
  a. don't know him very well **b.** trust him

8 A *revolution* usually indicates some kind of _____.
  a. great change **b.** intensified action

9 If you asked me what is the *ultimate* information source, I'd say the _____.
  a. public library **b.** Internet

B **Answer these questions. Share your answers with a partner.**

1 What habits are *crucial* to living a long and happy life?
2 What items besides clothes can be *custom* made?
3 Give some examples of *cutting-edge* technologies.
4 Think of an actor with a *distinctive* look. What makes him or her distinctive?
5 What shops or restaurants are the most *exclusive* in your country?
6 Describe the *interior* of your bedroom.
7 Who do you know who has a *reputation* for being honest?
8 What countries have had major political *revolutions*?
9 In your opinion, what is the *ultimate* dessert?

A Read the paragraph below, paying attention to the underlined words and phrases.

Hi David,

You missed a great party last night! I wore that red <u>dress</u> and it looked great! Jorge wore a tuxedo; he looked really handsome! The party was very festive; a lot of people were wearing the traditional <u>dress</u> of their countries. Harumi wore a Japanese kimono; Eun Mi had on a lovely Korean hanbok—it looked rather like a long skirt with a jacket. Alec was <u>well-dressed</u> as usual; he had on quite a handsome kilt and jacket. Antonio was co-hosting the party; he was <u>dressed in</u> black from head to toe—very impressive! Kenji and his girlfriend <u>dressed up</u> in costume for the occasion—I believe they were supposed to be a king and queen, but I'm not sure. Marie came with her boyfriend Eric; she was wearing a very stylish <u>dress suit</u> and red beret, but he was completely <u>underdressed</u> in shorts, sandals, and a T-shirt! But that's Eric; he always <u>dresses down</u> like that.

I'll tell you more when I see you this afternoon. I'm going to <u>get dressed</u> now. I'll see you in a couple of hours.

Naomi

Vocabulary Skill:
The Use of *Dress*

In this chapter, you've seen the word "dress" used in different ways. Depending on its part of speech, this word can have different meanings. It can also be combined with other words to talk about one's appearance and style.

B Match a word or phrase from the reading with a definition below. Also, write the part of speech in the chart. Check your answers with a partner.

Definition	Word or Phrase	Part of Speech
1 to put your clothes on		
2 wearing clothes that are too informal		
3 attractively dressed		
4 clothing or costume in general		
5 an article of clothing worn by women		
6 wear casual clothes		
7 to wear or be wearing		
8 put on formal or festive clothes		
9 formal item of clothing		

C Complete the statements and questions below with one of the words or phrases from A and B. Then, take turns asking and answering each with a partner.

1 Describe the clothes that you are _____ right now.
2 When do you _____—before or after you eat breakfast?
3 Describe your country or culture's traditional _____. Do you ever _____ in these clothes?
4 When was the last time you _____? Was it for a special occasion?

Real Life Skill:
Understanding Clothing Sizes

Countries all over the world have different ways of measuring clothing and shoe sizes. If you plan to visit another country, or are interested in shopping online for yourself or others, becoming familiar with some international clothing sizes can help you to make the right choices.

A Study the chart below. Are these ways of measuring clothes similar or identical to the measurements used in your country?

Women's Dresses/Blouses/Sweaters				
	U.S.	U.K.	Europe	Japan
XS	4	8	36	5
S	6	10	38-40	7
M	8	12	42-44	9
L	10	14	46-48	11
XL	12	16	50+	13

Men's Shirt Collar		
U.S./U.K.	Europe	Japan
14	36	36
$14^1/_2$	37	37
15	38	38
$15^1/_2$	39	39
16	40	40
$16^1/_2$	41	42

Women's Shoes			
U.S.	U.K.	Europe	Japan
4	3	36	21.5
5	4	37	22.5
6	5	38	23.5
7	6	39	24.5
8	7	40	25.5

Men's Shoes			
U.S.	U.K.	Europe	Japan
7	6	40	24.5
8	7	41	25.5
9	8	42	26.5
10	9	43	27.5
11	10	44	28.5

B Help the following people choose the right size clothes for the country they are living in. Write their measurements on the lines provided.

1 Kentaro is from Japan, but he is studying in the United Kingdom. His shirt size in Japan is 37, his shoe size 25.5. Shirt: _____ Shoes: _____
2 Birgit is from Switzerland, but she is living in the United States. Her European blouse size is 42, her shoe size is 40. Blouse: _____ Shoes: _____
3 Enrique is from Spain, and he's living in the United Kingdom. His shoe size is 43, his shirt size is 36. Shoes: _____ Shirt: _____
4 Anna is from the United States and is living in Japan. She needs to buy a pair of shoes. Her shoe size is 6 in the United States. Shoes: _____
5 Simon is from London and has just moved to Tokyo. He needs to buy a new dress shirt and shoes. His U.K. measurements are shirt size 15½ and shoe size 9. Shirt: _____ Shoes: _____

What Do You Think?

1 Do men in your country normally wear a suit and tie to work, or do they dress down in the workplace? Which do you prefer?
2 If someone looked at your wardrobe, what words would they use to describe you? Explain your answer.
3 What kind of clothes impress you? Describe a well-dressed man—what kind of clothes would he wear? What colors? Do the same for a woman.

Getting Ready

Discuss the following questions with a partner.

1 Match these names with the pictures above.

> **a.** great auk   **b.** thylacine (Tasmanian tiger)   **c.** moa   **d.** dodo

2 What do you think these four animals have in common?
3 Do you know any animal species whose numbers are diminishing?
4 What measures are being taken to protect animal species in your country?

Before You Read:
Valuing Wildlife

A Look at this list of reasons for protecting wildlife. Discuss them with a partner, then rank the reasons from 1 to 4 in order of importance.

Animals and plants make the world a more beautiful place. _____
Animals and plants can be used to create medicine. _____
Animals and plants hold many secrets that are important for us to learn. _____
Animals and plants have rights, and humans must respect them. _____

B Match the dangers to animals on the left with the solutions on the right.

Dangers to Wildlife	Solutions
1 unreasonable exploitation _____	a. programs to raise and release more animals into the wild
2 destruction of habitat _____	b. laws ensuring cleaner air and water
3 pollution _____	c. limits on the number of any animal species that can be captured or killed
4 slow rate of reproduction _____	d. creation of wildlife sanctuaries
5 domestic competition with non-native species _____	e. strict controls on the import and export of animals

Reading Skill:
Identifying Meaning from Context

To guess the meaning of an important but unfamiliar word in a passage, try the following strategy: First, look at the different parts of the word to see whether there are any clues to its meaning. Second, notice the word's part of speech. Third, look at the words and sentences around the new word for synonyms, antonyms, or a definition of the word.

A Read the sentences below. Which sentence best helps you understand the meaning of the word *threaten*? Explain your answer to a partner.

a. Pollution threatens.
b. Pollution threatens many animals and plants.
c. Pollution threatens many animals and plants by poisoning the land, water, and air.

B Find each *italicized* word below in the reading passage. Read the sentence the word is in and some of the surrounding sentences. Then choose the best definition.

1 In line 25, the word *factors* means _____.
   a. people with opinions   b. two or more numbers   c. reasons or causes
2 In line 26, the word *deforestation* means _____.
   a. the removal of trees   b. awareness of wildlife   c. competition
3 In line 46, the word *preserve* means to _____.
   a. destroy   b. protect   c. create

C Read through the passage again, then answer the questions that follow.

Endangered Species

Like individual animals, animal species[1] also eventually **die out**. It is estimated that, until the 18th century, one species disappeared from the Earth every four years. By the 19th century, this had increased to one species per year. By 1975, it was 1,000 species per year, and today animals are disappearing at the **appalling** rate of more than 40,000 species per year. Most species are threatened by pollution, habitat destruction, and unreasonable **exploitation** caused by humans. The International Union for Conservation of Nature has created a number of categories that describe the danger level of animal species:

- A species that has died out completely is called *extinct*. Examples are the dinosaurs and the dodo bird.
- Species that only live in zoos or on farms, etc., fall into the category *extinct in the wild*, for example, various horse species.
- A species is labeled *critically endangered* when it is in immediate danger of dying out completely. Its numbers are dangerously low, and it needs protection in order to survive. The Siberian tiger and the snow leopard are two examples.
- Species that have a high, but not immediate, risk of dying out are simply labeled *endangered*. The giant panda is a famous example.
- A *vulnerable* species is in less trouble than an endangered one, but its numbers are still certainly declining. The cheetah and the African elephant are vulnerable species.
- Animal species that aren't particularly endangered and have high numbers of individuals are labeled *less concern*.

There are many **factors** that can cause an animal or plant species to become endangered. The main cause of species endangerment is humanity's destruction of both water and land habitats. Deforestation and soil, air, and water pollution can all destroy habitat. This can then cause a large number of animals or plants to die. The critically endangered Sumatran orangutan has seen a 50% decline in its population over the last eight years as farmers clear more and more forests for agriculture.

Another cause of endangerment is the unreasonable exploitation of animals. Uncontrolled hunting of whales in the last century, for example, resulted in many whale species becoming critically endangered. The very high **demand** for animal parts for use in certain foods or medicines is another example. The horn of the rhinoceros can be sold at a high price in some places where it is thought to be medicinal: a price so high that people will kill the animals even though it is against the law.

Introducing a non-native species to an environment can also cause species endangerment. A native species is one that develops naturally in a particular area, and has done so for a long time. A non-native

species might be introduced into a new environment by humans, either **intentionally** or by accident. The brown tree snake, unknowingly introduced by cargo[2] ships stopping at Guam, has managed to kill off ten of the eleven species of birds native to the island's forests. In Florida, large pet snakes such as the anaconda
40 and the python have been released into the large Everglades swamp. The snakes have been quite successful, and now compete with and even threaten the swamp's alligators.

Organizations such as the World Wildlife Fund and the International Union for Conservation of Nature try to raise **awareness** of threatened animals and plants. These organizations work with government agencies to save threatened or endangered species, and to make new laws that will protect these species.
45 Many of these plans work, but some do not. Public awareness of this issue is important. To preserve the quality of our lives and the lives of future generations, we must also protect plant and animal species now and in the future.

[1]**species** a group of animals or plants that are very similar and can reproduce together
[2]**cargo** the contents of a ship, plane, truck, etc., that are being transported

Reading Comprehension:
Check Your Understanding

A Decide whether the following statements about the reading are true (T) or false (F). If you check (✔) false, correct the statement to make it true.

	T	F
1 The author of the reading passage probably wrote it to help raise awareness about declining animal populations.		
2 The cause of most recent animal extinctions is nature.		
3 There has been a 50% decline in the habitat of the Sumatran orangutan.		
4 Humans unknowingly introduced brown tree snakes to Guam.		
5 Uncontrolled hunting resulted in the extinction of many whale species.		

B Match the animals on the left with the categories from the reading on the right.

1 African elephant _____   **a.** extinct
2 dodo _____   **b.** extinct in the wild
3 horses _____   **c.** critically endangered
4 Siberian tiger _____   **d.** endangered
5 giant panda _____   **e.** vulnerable

C Critical Thinking

Discuss these questions with a partner.

1 For what purpose did the International Union for Conservation of Nature probably create its list of six categories?
2 Do you think most people are concerned about endangered species? Why or why not?
3 What are some ways that we can help in the fight to save threatened species?

A For each group, circle the word that does not belong. The words in *italics* are vocabulary items from the reading.

1 *appalling*	exclusive	high class	elite
2 understanding	reputation	*awareness*	knowledge
3 command	*demand*	need	request
4 *die out*	disappear	vanish	dye
5 living	surviving	*extinct*	alive
6 *factor*	reason	cause	focus
7 mistakenly	*intentionally*	accidentally	inadvertently
8 removal	elimination	*exploitation*	taking away
9 sacred	*vulnerable*	weak	helpless

B Complete the sentences below using the words in *italics* from A. Be sure to use the correct form of the word.

1 Unable to adapt to the new conditions of life, the dinosaurs became
_____.

2 If public _____ about the cruelty of fur is raised, more people will wear synthetic imitations of fur instead of the real thing.

3 By imitating the sound of a weakened and _____ deer, the hunters attracted a hungry Siberian tiger.

4 Two _____ in the extinction of the dodo were unreasonable exploitation and the introduction of non-native species.

5 The hunter said he shot the animal accidentally; the police think he did it _____ in order to sell it for a high price.

6 Thirty elephants were killed with machine guns in a wildlife sanctuary in a(n) _____ incident of illegal hunting.

7 Because it was against their religion to have children, the believers slowly
_____.

8 When the _____ for a species of animal for pets is high, they can be sold at a high price.

9 The American bison nearly went extinct due to unreasonable _____ of it for meat and leather.

Vocabulary Skill:

The Prefixes *ex-*, *en-*, and *em-*

In this chapter you read the word "exploitation." This word begins with the prefix "ex-," meaning "out of" or "from within." You also read the word "endangered," which begins with the prefix "en-," meaning "(to put) into" or "to cover." When "en-" comes before "b" or "p," it changes to "em-."

A **What do you think the following words mean? Use them to complete the sentences below. Use a dictionary to help you.**

> enclose   embark   extend   embrace   exterior

1 Do you see that sign over there that says "_____"? We get on the ship there.
2 After the car accident, Mark had to wear a cast and was unable to _____ his arm.
3 In some countries, people _____ and kiss each other on both cheeks when they meet.
4 When you mail the phone bill today, don't forget to _____ the payment in the envelope.
5 This building's _____ hasn't been painted in years and it looks terrible.

B **Now use *em-*, *en-*, or *ex-* to complete the words in the sentences below. Check your answers with a partner.**

1 When Arthur gave Jill a new car, she _____pressed her thanks by hugging him.
2 Thirty minutes after the fire started, the building was completely _____veloped in flames.
3 The bullet is _____bedded in the door, and the police can't seem to remove it.
4 Sylvie works for a company that _____ports wine from France to Japan.
5 Rupert had the date of his wedding _____graved on the inside of his wedding ring.

Chapter 2: Bring Back the Woolly Mammoth?   Unit 3

Discuss these questions with a partner.

1 Have you seen the movie *Jurassic Park*?
2 What was the basic plot of that movie?
3 In the movie, how were they able to bring dinosaurs back from extinction?
4 Do you think a real dinosaur park could be created? Would it be a good idea?

A **Look at the statements below. Write "M" next to the statement that you think is the main idea of each paragraph. Share your answers with a partner.**

1 **Paragraph 2**
   a. Nobody is serious about bringing back extinct species. _____
   b. There are a number of extinct species that might be revived. _____
2 **Paragraph 4**
   a. There are two different ways to go about reviving extinct species. _____
   b. Sex cells of the extinct species can be used to revive it. _____
3 **Paragraph 5**
   a. Some scientists believe that extinct species will never be brought back. _____
   b. There are still quite a few problems preventing extinct species revival. _____
4 **Paragraph 6**
   a. It may be wrong to bring back extinct species. _____
   b. An example of an extinct species would be one-of-a-kind and lonely. _____

B **Scan the reading passage to see whether you were correct. Discuss your answers with a partner.**

C **Now read the passage again, then complete the questions that follow.**

Reading Skill:

Identifying Main Ideas within Paragraphs

Many paragraphs are constructed around a main idea. This idea is usually presented in a sentence within the paragraph. Quickly finding the main idea will increase your speed of reading and comprehension.

Bring Back the Woolly Mammoth?

In the 1993 film *Jurassic Park,* several species of dinosaurs have been brought back to life using DNA millions of years old. The dinosaurs are placed in an animal theme park as a tourist attraction. However, when a group of scientists arrives for a visit, the dinosaurs escape and attack them. After many scary **encounters**, only a few of the visitors remain alive.

The story is of course fiction, but it reflects recent advances in genetic engineering which are getting ever closer to reality. At this point no one really suggests bringing back dinosaurs, but there are a number of serious proposals to **revive** extinct species. The animals on this possible comeback list include the woolly mammoth, an elephant-like creature that **wandered** the plains of Siberia; the moa, a giant flightless bird from New Zealand; the thylacine, a dog-like hunter also known as the Tasmanian tiger because of the dark stripes down its back; and the bucardo, a mountain goat from Spain.

These animals had very little in common and in most cases lived **eras** apart. The woolly mammoth, for example, died many thousands of years ago while the bucardo became extinct only around the year 2000. But, all these species lived at the same time as humans, and humans have been largely responsible for their destruction. So it seems somehow **fitting** that we are now thinking of reviving them.

Scientists have proposed reviving an extinct species using one of two possible methods. In the first method, sex cells (sperm or eggs) are obtained from the extinct animal and are used to **fertilize** the sex cells of a closely related living relative in a laboratory. For example, sperm from a woolly mammoth could be used to fertilize an egg from a modern-day elephant. The fertilized egg would then be placed in the womb of a live female elephant where it would live and grow until it is ready to be born. The second method involves a type of cloning. In cloning, the DNA of one individual replaces the DNA of another. In the woolly mammoth example, scientists could inject DNA from a mammoth into an egg cell from an elephant. The cloned egg cell would then be placed into a living elephant and allowed to develop in the same way as a fertilized egg.

Many difficulties remain before it will be possible to revive an extinct species by either method. In fact, some scientists believe that because of all the problems, species revival will never happen. One of the major challenges is to obtain enough high-quality DNA from an extinct species to **conduct** an experiment. While it is theoretically possible to preserve genetic material for thousands of years under ideal conditions, these conditions are very hard to find in real life. For example, researchers have obtained a number of samples of mammoth DNA, but none have been usable. And the cloning procedure presents its own problems. Scientists have been able to clone only a few species of animals, and most cloned creatures are short-lived and **frail**.

And there is a final, **ethical** consideration. Even if we learn how to reproduce an example of an extinct species, that individual could never have a normal life. Its natural environment is most likely gone, and it would have no parents to show it how to behave as a member of its species. So it would remain a curiosity, and probably live out its life in a zoo. People question whether it would be ethical to revive one of nature's creatures for such a purpose.

40

A **How much do you remember from the reading? Choose the best answer for each of the questions or statements below.**

1 What is the main idea of the reading?
   a. Reviving extinct animals may or may not be possible, and it may not be right.
   b. Reviving extinct animals is science fiction, and it will probably never be possible.
   c. Reviving extinct animals is quite possible, and it will happen in the near future.
2 What was the main cause for the extinction of the thylacine, the moa, the mammoth, and the bucardo?
   a. changing weather   **b.** not enough food   **c.** humans
3 Which of the following is NOT a method for reviving extinct species?
   a. fertilization of the egg of an existing species with the sperm of an extinct one
   b. the cloning of an extinct species
   c. finding a dinosaur egg and warming it under the right conditions
4 What is true about cloned animals?
   a. They are usually very healthy.
   b. They are often weak and frail.
   c. They look quite different from other members of their species.
5 According to the article, reviving extinct species _____.
   a. is something we should do as soon as possible
   b. will allow us to return many animal populations to the wild
   c. is a highly difficult process that may not ever occur

B **Decide whether the following statements about the reading are true (T) or false (F), or whether the information is not given (NG). If you check (✔) false, correct the statement to make it true.**

	T	F	NG
1 There are many serious proposals to revive extinct species.			
2 The woolly mammoth lived on the plains of Siberia.			
3 One example of the thylacine was produced by cloning, but it died.			
4 Researchers have obtained usable samples of mammoth DNA.			
5 The natural habitats of many extinct species are likely gone.			

C Critical Thinking

Discuss these questions with a partner.

1 If scientists were able to revive the woolly mammoth from extinction, should they be released into the wild or kept in zoos? Why?

2 The reading mentions several reasons why reviving extinct animals might not be a good idea. What are some reasons for reviving extinct animals?

Vocabulary Comprehension:
Word Definitions

A Match each vocabulary item on the left with a definition on the right.

1 conduct _____   a. unexpected meeting
2 encounter _____   b. period of time
3 era _____   c. appropriate; suitable
4 ethical _____   d. weak and unhealthy
5 fertilize _____   e. to walk around without a clear direction
6 fitting _____   f. to cause to live again
7 frail _____   g. right, not wrong; regarding right and wrong
8 revive _____   h. to cause an egg or seed to start developing
9 wander _____   i. to perform a particular activity, such as an
                         investigation, an experiment, or a survey

B Complete the sentences below using the vocabulary from A. Be sure to use the correct form of the word.

1 In *Jurassic Park*, a scientist _____ dinosaurs from extinction with appalling consequences.

2 The escaped monkey _____ around the interior of the laboratory, not knowing where to go or what to do.

3 If the egg of an animal isn't _____, it will never grow.

4 In the wild, animals that are _____ are the most vulnerable to attack.

5 The teacher is going to _____ a class survey to find our level of awareness about endangered species.

6 There are many _____ questions about cloning, and particularly about human cloning.

7 It is _____ that the most endangered animals should be those most carefully protected by laws.

8 The scientist was overjoyed after his _____ with an animal thought to have died out.

9 During the disco _____, platform shoes and synthetic fabrics were trendy.

A What do you think the following words mean? Complete the sentences below with the words. Be sure to use the correct form of the words.

> computerize fertilize hospitalize idolize
> industrialize legalize deodorize

1 Thousands of teen girls _____ that rock star. They can't resist his allure.
2 Due to the air pollution during the hot and humid summer, many old people were _____ with breathing problems.
3 Drinking alcohol used to be illegal in the United States. It was _____ in 1933.
4 _____ countries can produce higher quantities of products than those that continue to produce goods by hand.
5 This new cleaner claims to _____ carpets that smell bad.
6 Our company used to have rows and rows of filing cabinets to store information on paper before our office systems were _____.
7 For fruit trees to produce fruit, it is crucial that there be bees and other insects to visit the flowers and _____ the fruit.

B Add the suffix *-ize* to the words in the box and use them to complete the sentences. Be sure to add *-ize* to the root word.

> modern sanitary final energy colony demon

1 A cup of coffee before a test always _____ me.
2 I can't show you the party plans until I _____ them.
3 You can use alcohol or iodine to _____ a wound.
4 In just a few years the country's electrical and road systems were _____.
5 Most of North America was _____ by England, France, and Spain.
6 The hated leader was _____ in the newspapers after the revolution.

Vocabulary Skill:
The Suffix *-ize*

In this chapter you saw the word "fertilize," meaning "to make fertile." This is one of the uses of the suffix "-ize," a very important suffix in English that can turn nouns and adjectives into verbs. In British English, "-ize" is also spelled "-ise."

Real Life Skill:
Dictionary Usage:
Choosing the Right Word

In English, there are many words or phrases that are similar in meaning but are not exactly the same. In a good English-English dictionary, there will often be usage notes that compare the word or phrase with another, or explain how the word or phrase is used. Using these notes can help you choose the correct word or phrase.

A Read the dictionary entries below. Then, explain to a partner how the words "dead" and "extinct," "exotic" and "foreign" are similar and different.

> **dead** *adj.* no longer living, lifeless *I think the woman has been dead for about two hours.*
> **ex•tinct** *adj.* something that is no longer in existence, specifically a type of animal, plant, or idea *Dinosaurs became extinct about 60 million years ago.*
> **ex•ot•ic** *adj.* different, strange, foreign, usually in an interesting or exciting way *Carmen prepared an exotic dish from southern Spain that was delicious.*
> **for•eign** *adj.* located outside one's native country or area; non-native, different *Hiroko speaks Japanese and two foreign languages.*

B Complete the sentences below with one of the words from A.

1 I've traveled all over my own country and, in addition, have visited five _____ countries.
2 There were once many dodo birds on the island of Mauritius in the Indian Ocean. Since the late 1800s, though, the bird has been _____.
3 I thought that Cary Grant, the actor, was still alive, but someone told me that he's been _____ for more than ten years.
4 Many people think the white tiger is a(n) _____ and beautiful animal.

C Think of a synonym for a new word or phrase you learned in this unit. Can the word or phrase and its synonym be used in exactly the same way? Use your dictionary to help you.

What Do You Think?

1 What can you do to help endangered animals?
2 If human beings ever go to live on other planets, do you think we should take animals with us? Which ones?
3 Some animals are not threatened with extinction, even in a world full of humans. Which animals are these, and why are they so successful?
4 Create a poster that tells people about an endangered species. In the poster, give the following information: an estimate of the number of individuals of the species that are still alive; factors causing the species to die out; what people can do to prevent the species from becoming extinct.

Fluency Strategy: *DRTA*

When you begin reading you should ask yourself, "Why am I reading this? What do I hope to learn?" Reading comprehension improves when you read with a purpose. **D**irected **R**eading **T**hinking **A**ctivity (DRTA) is a method that will help you to read critically and purposefully. Each stage of the DRTA procedure has four steps: Predicting, Reading, Proving, and Reasoning

Predicting

Look at the photo, and read the title and the first sentence from the passage on the next page. Make predictions (or *hypotheses*) about what you will read about in the passage. For example, what do you think "ecotourism" involves? What kind of effects might it have?

_____

_____

Ecotourism

Ecotourism is a combination of *ecology* (a system of living things) and *tourism*.

Reading

Now read the first two paragraphs of the passage. As you read, consider whether your predictions were accurate.

Proving

When you have finished reading the first two paragraphs, discuss what you learned with a partner. Read aloud the parts of the passage that relate to your predictions. Were your predictions accurate? Do you need to revise them?

Reasoning

Now, based on what you have learned so far, make new predictions. What will you read about in the next two paragraphs? Why do you think so?

_____

_____

Continue with steps 2–4 above until you have read the whole passage. Then, with a partner, summarize the main points you have learned about "ecotourism."

_____

_____

Ecotourism

Ecotourism is a combination of *ecology* (the study of systems of living things) and *tourism*. The International Ecotourism Society defines ecotourism as "responsible travel to natural areas that conserves
5 the environment and improves the well-being of the local people." Actually, ecotourism can mean travel to far-off places of great natural beauty, but not always in a responsible way. It's big business, and the allure of money can cause people to think about profits first.
10 While ecotourism offers benefits for people and ecosystems, it leaves ecosystems open to negative effects, too.

Costa Rica, once a Spanish colony, and independent since 1821, has an ecotourism industry worth over one billion dollars yearly, and thousands of jobs have been created. Nearly 21 percent of the land is now protected national parks, largely thanks to ecotourism. Nonetheless,
15 due to the number of people visiting the country's natural places, some damage to the ecosystem has occurred.

While tourists can have a negative impact on ecosystems, the same areas might have been totally destroyed by industries such as farming, logging, or mining were there no ecotourism industry. Instead, sanctuaries have been created, keeping the ecosystem protected. And, by
20 visiting beautiful rainforests and seeing rare animals, visitors get a sense of their value, and of gratitude for them. Tour guides can also be educators who train people to love and care for the environment. Visitors can take these lessons with them to their home countries.

Unfortunately, while their effect may not be noticeable in the off-season, the constant procession of visitors in the high season can be damaging. At one national park in Costa Rica,
25 wild monkeys now feed on garbage left by the tourists. Furthermore, ecotourists tend to seek out places with the rarest animals and plants, pressuring the most delicate of living things.

Controlling abuses isn't easy. Corruption can lead officials to tolerate ecological damage. For example, a large resort facility, normally not allowed near a sanctuary, might be allowed if the company pays enough money to certain people in the government. Limited resources are
30 another issue. Areas of forests and beaches that would require an army to protect are often watched by several employees.

It is easy to be critical of the ecotourism industry, but it is important to be positive as well. Ecotourism can never be "pure." We can't expect zero negative effects on the ecosystem. It is also unrealistic to think that humans won't go anywhere accessible to them. If protection efforts
35 are maintained and intensified, those remaining places of undisturbed nature may be stressed, but they won't be destroyed.

Check how well you understood the passage by answering the following questions.

1 Which statement best summarizes the author's point of view?
   a. Ecotourism is a damaging trend that must be stopped.
   b. Ecotourism is a way of protecting natural places.
   c. Ecotourism causes some damage, but on the whole it benefits ecosystems.
   d. Ecotourism will most likely become less popular in the future.

2 Which change has NOT occurred in Costa Rica since the introduction of ecotourism?
   a. Thousands of ecotourism-related jobs have been created.
   b. National parks have been created.
   c. Some monkeys have started feeding on garbage.
   d. Costa Rica became independent from Spain.

3 What is the main idea of paragraph 3?
   a. Ecotourism threatens to destroy rainforests as would farming, logging, and mining.
   b. While ecotourism damages them somewhat, it also protects natural places from destruction.
   c. Tour guides need to educate tourists on the dangers of farming, logging, and mining.
   d. Rare animals need to be protected from visitors taking them home to their countries.

4 According to paragraph 5, why is it difficult to control abuses of ecotourism?
   a. Too many sanctuaries are being created.
   b. Officials are too few and can be too tolerant.
   c. Not many people are interested in jobs controlling ecotourism abuses.
   d. There is a lot of money available to build resorts.

5 Into which paragraph could the following sentence best be inserted?: *In this way, the children of future generations can learn respect for nature.*
   a. Paragraph 3
   b. Paragraph 4
   c. Paragraph 5
   d. Paragraph 6

6 The word "corruption" in line 27 is closest in meaning to _____ .
   a. illegal activity
   b. tolerance
   c. government control
   d. management

7 Why does the author probably think it is easy to be critical of the ecotourism industry?
   a. because wildlife is very easy to protect
   b. because it doesn't make very much money
   c. because it takes advantage of nature for profit
   d. because it can't create enough jobs for local people

Self Check

Write a short answer to each of the following questions.

1. Have you ever used the DRTA method before?

   Yes   No   *I'm not sure.*

2. Will you practice DRTA in your reading outside of English class?

   Yes   No   *I'm not sure.*

3. Do you think DRTA is helpful? Why or why not?

   _____

   _____

4. Which of the six reading passages in units 1–3 did you enjoy most? Why?

   _____

   _____

5. Which of the six reading passages in units 1–3 was easiest? Which was most difficult? Why?

   _____

   _____

6. What have you read in English outside of class recently?

   _____

   _____

7. Do you usually think about your purpose for reading before you read something? If yes, how, or if not, why not?

   _____

   _____

8. How will you try to improve your reading fluency from now on?

   _____

   _____

Review Reading 1: Modern Fashion Trends

Fluency Practice

Time yourself as you read through the passage. Try to read as fluently as you can. Record your time in the Reading Rate Chart on page 208. Then answer the questions on the following page.

http://www.ASR_fashiontalk.com

Modern Fashion Trends ●●●●●●●●●●●●●●●

Fashions today are changing faster than ever, influenced by a variety of forces. Clearly, many of these changes are dictated by music-related cultural movements like hip-hop, boy bands,
5   or grunge. The stars of these music genres are idolized, and their clothing choices directly influence the fashion of their fans who wish to imitate them. Another undeniable influence on what fashion is "cool" is technology. Technology
10   that can be worn is now and will become an ever more important part of the "look" of fashionable young people. There are many other trends, among them retro or vintage fashion, and so-called disposable fashion.

15   The hip-hop revolution of the 1970s and '80s brought a whole new look to our attention, a look for an American city culture that made a statement. Modern hip-hop clothes, however, are often produced by successful, big-name fashion designers, and are quite expensive. In fact, many hip-hop artists such as Eminem, Kanye West, and others have their own lines of hip-hop clothing. The essentials of the modern hip-hop look are gold chains, boots or *kicks* (slang for sneakers),
20   a bandana tied around the head, often with a cap on top, and large T-shirts. The baggy look of decades gone by has been replaced by a look that includes polo shirts and tighter denim jeans.

Another trendy, cutting-edge movement in the world of fashion is technology you wear, and the blending of technology with clothing. More and more, people are afraid to be without a cell phone, a computer, or Internet access at any time of the day or night. Wearable technology helps

25 people keep those crucial connections to the world open, while at the same time giving them a distinctive look. Clip-on MP3 players with headphones, "hands-free" phones and earpieces, and personal digital assistants (PDAs) are just a few of the ever more visible portable technology components that are part of the look. The ultimate in technology-friendly clothing, the solar-powered jacket can now provide the electricity needed to keep all these gadgets running.

30 The retro or vintage style of clothing brings trends from past decades back into style. Grunge was a style of music born in the Seattle area in the 1990s. Grunge fans stayed away from synthetic fabrics, preferring flannel shirts, stone-washed jeans, and rock T-shirts. They preferred dark colors like greens, dark purples, or browns. For footwear, grunge fans wore Dr. Martens-style shoes and boots or high-top sneakers. Although the grunge music craze also ended in the '90s, a modern
35 retro fashion trend is taking its cue from grunge-era clothing. Modern grunge fashion is similar in many ways, but it's much less baggy and sloppy than it was in the '90s.

H&M, a chain of Swedish clothing stores, is the name most often connected with the new trend in youth fashion known as disposable fashion. It's clothing so cheap that you don't mind buying it and wearing it only several times, perhaps, before discarding it. Disposable fashion is often
40 brightly colored and stylish, but low in price. The trend, which reportedly started in Japan, grew popular in Europe, and is taking root in America, shows no signs of slowing down.

What will the future of fashion look like? Well, technology is sure to remain a growing part of fashion, with ever smaller cell phones, computers, PDAs, and other wearable gadgets. All around the world, more people are wearing hip-hop fashions than ever before. No longer exclusive to
45 urban youth or even the United States, hip-hop will remain a popular global fashion for years to come. Retro fashions from the '80s and '90s, including the grunge look, seem to be growing in popularity, and disposable fashion is a big hit that won't end soon. And, I'm sure that we will see new fashion surprises as music, fashion, and technology move forward together into the future.

642 words   Time taken _____

Reading Comprehension

1 What is the main purpose of the passage?
   a. to explain why certain fashions are popular internationally
   b. to show the best fashions to wear in order to look "cool"
   c. to inform us about current and future fashion trends
   d. to explain the history of certain fashion trends

2 Which fashion trend is NOT mentioned in the article?
   a. grunge
   b. hip-hop
   c. retro
   d. business casual

3 According to paragraph 2, how has hip-hop changed?
   a. Hip-hop clothes are now sold by big-name designers and are less baggy.
   b. Boots used to be popular, but now *kicks* are worn.
   c. Hip-hop moved from other countries to the United States.
   d. The baggy hip-hop look has replaced tighter jeans and polo shirts.

4 What trend has been brought back by the retro style?
   a. hip-hop
   b. wearable technology
   c. grunge
   d. disposable fashion

5 Which fashion trend would most likely be the most popular with someone who didn't have much money to spend?
   a. hip-hop
   b. wearable technology
   c. retro
   d. disposable fashion

6 Why might disposable fashion clothes not go well with the grunge look?
   a. because disposable fashion is cheap
   b. because grunge is from Seattle
   c. because disposable fashion is often brightly colored
   d. because the grunge music craze ended in the '90s

7 According to paragraph 6, which of the following is a likely future trend?
   a. Wearable technology will involve smaller devices.
   b. Hip-hop will become exclusive to the United States.
   c. Retro fashions will go out of style.
   d. Disposable fashions will increase in price.

Review Reading 2: Endangered Animal Success Stories

Fluency Practice

Time yourself as you read through the passage. Try to read as fluently as you can. Record your time in the Reading Rate Chart on page 208. Then answer the questions on the following page.

Endangered Animal Success Stories

In 2006, the United States government declared May 11 to be Endangered Species Day. This day was created to encourage people to raise their awareness and understanding of the problem of endangered

5　species. Indeed, the government has shown itself to be a true friend of endangered species. In 1973, the United States government passed into law the Endangered Species Act. Its three major goals were as follows: to protect plants and animals from

10　extinction by listing them as endangered; to preserve the habitat of these species; and to help populations of listed species recover. Today, we celebrate dozens of success stories of animals brought back from near extinction. Here are three such success stories.

15　It is fitting that we begin with the story of the bald eagle, the national symbol of the United States. Before the arrival of the Europeans in North America, it is estimated that the population of bald eagles in the United States, excluding Alaska, was about 100,000 birds. By 1963, the population had dropped to less than 1,000 individuals—an appalling trend. Hunting was certainly a major factor in this decline, as was the destruction of habitat, but another factor

20　was a chemical used in the control of insects, DDT. It had a strange effect on the eagles' eggs. It made their shells very thin so that they broke easily, and the baby birds inside were frail.

The single most important factor in the recovery of the bald eagle was a 1972 ban on DDT. Being listed as an endangered species gave the birds additional protection. Bald eagle populations are now carefully watched, and baby eagles are raised under human protection

25　to be later released into the wild. Thanks to these efforts, the number of eagles in the United States, excluding Alaska, has grown to about 14,000.

Another classic symbol of North American wildlife is the grizzly bear. In the era before the Europeans arrived, more than 50,000 grizzlies wandered the American West. Today that number is closer to 1,000. Because grizzly bears have babies at a very slow rate, it takes

30　many years for the population to grow.

Most of the grizzly bears in the United States, excluding Alaska, live in the protection of Yellowstone and Glacier National Parks. Hunting them has been completely outlawed. As bear populations grow, it becomes very important to prevent encounters between humans and bears: 20 to 40 bears are killed each year in such encounters. Garbage management is
35 an important factor in keeping bears away from humans.

In the Florida Keys, a chain of islands off the coast of Florida, there lives a small population of tiny deer called Key deer. They once lived on a number of islands, but they have gradually been limited to mainly one. The Key deer very nearly died out—at one point there were only 25 remaining. In the past, hunting was a big problem. Recently, deer are rarely killed
40 intentionally, but exploitation of their island's land for homes, roads, and tourism has destroyed much of their habitat. Automobiles also kill a number of deer each year.

The Key deer was one of the first animals to be listed as endangered. In 1957, a sanctuary was created for the deer. There, a staff conducts health checks on them. Thanks to these efforts, their population has returned to about 500.

45 We hope that the government continues to be on the side of endangered species. Each unique species enriches our environment and is certainly worth protecting. By protecting endangered species, we also express our respect for the place in which we live. At the same time, we present a gift of great value to future generations of people.

615 words   Time taken _____

Reading Comprehension

1 What was the author's main purpose in writing this passage?
 a. to celebrate government successes in helping endangered animals
 b. to instruct people in the United States about how to save animals
 c. to point out the causes of animal endangerment
 d. to encourage people to send money to help animals

2 What is NOT mentioned in the passage as a goal of the Endangered Species Act?
 a. listing animals and plants as endangered
 b. preserving plant and animal habitat
 c. assisting endangered species populations to grow
 d. creating national parks

3 What was the single most destructive factor for bald eagle populations?
 a. hunting
 b. loss of habitat
 c. the use of DDT
 d. the naturally slow rate of producing baby eagles

4 According to the passage, for which animal is garbage management important?
 a. the bald eagle
 b. the grizzly bear
 c. the Key deer
 d. all of the above

5 According to the passage, what kills a number of Key deer each year?
 a. grizzly bears
 b. bald eagles
 c. DDT
 d. cars

6 What is today's population of Key deer?
 a. about 25
 b. about 500
 c. about 1,000
 d. about 14,000

7 According to the passage, why is it important to protect endangered species?
 a. They enrich our environment.
 b. It shows our respect for our environment.
 c. We can leave a gift for future people.
 d. all of the above

Getting Ready

Discuss the following questions with a partner.

1. What has happened to the people pictured above?
2. Finish this sentence: *If I won a million dollars, I would . . .*
3. Is there a lottery in your country? How much money can you win?
4. Do you think having a lot of money can guarantee happiness? Why or why not?

Before You Read:
Money Knowledge

A **Look at the list of sentences below. Match each cause with an effect.**

Cause (reason)

1 This area has become very popular among home buyers in recent years.
2 Many game shows now offer more than $1 million in prize money.
3 Danny spent all his lottery winnings within a few weeks.
4 Yong-jin won the top prize on last week's *Win a Million!* show.
5 The cost of education has increased recently.

Effect (result)

_____ **a.** Housing is now very expensive here.
_____ **b.** He's taking his family on a round-the-world vacation.
_____ **c.** Many students have to work part-time to pay for their schooling.
_____ **d.** The popularity of game shows has increased in recent years.
_____ **e.** Now he doesn't have any of the money left.

B **Write five sentences combining the causes and the effects. Use "because," "due to (the fact that)," "as a result," "so," and "therefore."**

Example: Housing is now very expensive here because this area has become popular among home buyers in recent years.

Reading Skill:
Identifying Cause and Effect

> Words and phrases such as "because," "due to (the fact that)," "as a result," "so," and "therefore" are used to show a cause-and-effect relationship; that is, they signal that one thing (the cause) makes another thing (the effect) happen. Recognizing words and phrases that signal cause and effect can help you better understand and organize the information in a reading passage.

A **Skim the passage. Then write the Effect (result) of each Cause (reason) below. Compare your answers with a partner.**

Cause (reason)	Effect (result)
1 The density of the population has increased, but the supply of available homes is smaller.	Housing has become very expensive.
2 People want to be closer to their workplace.	
3 Prices have gone up, but the value of money has gone down.	
4 Many older people are living longer.	

B **Notice what words and phrases you used to understand the cause-and-effect relationships in A and discuss them with a partner.**

C **Now read the passage again, then answer the questions that follow.**

What Does a Million Dollars Buy?

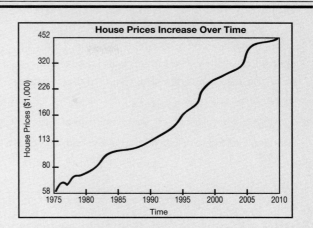

People often think that having a million dollars would make all their dreams come true. There are TV game shows that give people the chance to become millionaires. Many people on these
5 shows probably believe that with this money, they could do anything or go anywhere. In reality, "a million" may not really be that much money. When asked the question "What would you do with a million dollars?" most people tend to give
10 similar answers: "Quit my job," "Buy my dream house," or "Go traveling." Twenty years ago, it was possible to **realize** these dreams. However, things are not so easy today.

In many industrialized countries, the **cost of**
15 **living** is higher than ever. One of the main reasons for this is demand. Over the last twenty years, for example, housing prices in many of the world's cities have **soared**. The main reason is that the population has become very **dense**
20 in certain areas, but there is a smaller **supply** of available housing there for sale or rent. For example, in the U.S., the average housing price in the state of Arizona in 1995 was approximately $160,000. The average price in 2006 was
25 $400,000. Now, because more people live in the area, the cost of **property** has risen dramatically.

Apartments in many city centers are also more expensive now than in the past. In the recent past, people often moved from a city center to
30 other city neighborhoods or the suburbs in order to escape overcrowding and noise. Today, people want to be closer to their workplace, and many are now moving back into the city center. As a result, living in or near this area costs more than
35 ever. Apartments in London's Mayfair district or in Manhattan in New York City often sell for over a million dollars. Many of these modern apartment complexes have indoor swimming pools or movie theaters that allow people to relax or exercise
40 without leaving their building.

Inflation is another important reason for the rise in the cost of living. Over the last 150 years, as prices have gone up, the value of money has gone down, so we now need more money to buy things.
45 In 1913, for example, $50,000 had about as much buying power as $1 million does today. Of course, people now earn more money than they did 150 years ago, but they also spend more on necessities such as food, medicine, and housing.

50 In order to live well after you stop working, you should begin saving for retirement early. Experts suggest that after you retire, you will need 75 percent to 80 percent of your salary to live on every month. In other words, if you make $3,000
55 per month while working, you will need between $2,250 and $2,400 per month to live on during retirement. This **calculation** assumes that you have

no mortgage[1] on a house to continue paying, or any other major expenses. However, many retired
60 people now rent their housing, and so they will pay more money in housing costs over time. Older people now also have to spend more on health care because they live longer; many people in industrialized countries now live into their eighties
65 or nineties.

Due to increased demand for housing, higher inflation, and longer **life expectancy,** a million may not be enough to live on. Of course, where you live and how long you live will influence
70 how much a million dollars can buy. To be able to retire early, travel the world, and build your dream home, you may have to appear on that game show and win more than once!

[1]**mortgage** a long-term loan from a bank, for buying property

Reading Comprehension:
Check Your Understanding

A Complete the sentences with the correct answer, then discuss your answers with a partner.

1 The author indicates that a million dollars may not be enough to _____.

2 In 1995, the cost of an average home in Arizona was _____; in 2006, it cost _____.

3 In the past, people moved out of the city center because of _____.

4 In order to live well after retirement, a person should _____ early in life.

B Decide whether the following statements about the reading are true (T) or false (F), or whether the information is not given (NG). If you check (✔) false, correct the statement to make it true.

	T	F	NG
1 A million dollars isn't as valuable as it used to be.			
2 People who move out of Arizona can find less expensive housing.			
3 Between 1975 and 2006, the price of housing in Arizona never fell.			
4 Many people in industrialized countries now live into their 70s.			

C Critical Thinking

Discuss these questions with a partner.

1 Looking at the chart in the reading, can we say about where housing costs will be in 2010?

2 If you lived in a place where housing prices were soaring like Arizona, what kind of house would you buy and where?

3 At what age would you like to retire? Do you think you'll have enough money by then?

A Look at the list of words from the reading. Match each word or phrase with a definition on the right.

1 calculate _____
2 cost of living _____
3 dense _____
4 inflation _____
5 life expectancy _____
6 property _____
7 realize _____
8 soar _____
9 supply _____

a. to go very high, usually by flying
b. an amount of something that is available for use
c. things that one owns; often used to talk about one's house or land
d. thick; close together
e. the average number of years to live
f. to make something happen or to make it real; to fulfill
g. things that one must pay for regularly, e.g., rent, food, bills
h. a continuing increase in prices over time
i. to do math; to figure out

B Complete the sentences using the words from A. Be sure to use the correct form of the word.

1 Can you use your computer to _____ how much my _____ in Arizona will be worth in 2015?

2 This year I hope to _____ my dream of _____ in the sky in a hang glider.

3 Experts say that when a country's money _____ is very high, that means that things start to get more expensive and _____ is the result.

4 You should stop smoking! It decreases your _____ and increases your _____!

5 The population is so _____ here. An average of ten people live in each apartment.

Vocabulary Skill:

The Prefixes *in-*, *im-*, *il-*, and *ir-*

In this chapter you read the word "inflation." This word begins with the prefix "in-," meaning "in" or "into." The prefix "in-" can also mean "not." When the prefix "in-" comes before the letter "l," the prefix changes to "il-." Before "m" or "p," it changes to "im-." Before "r," it changes to "ir-."

A **What do you think the following words mean? Complete the sentences below with the words.**

> install   illogical   illustration   immature
> inseparable   irresponsible   import

1 Use an _____ to explain new words. This will make it easier for beginning students to understand.
2 It was _____ of you to stay out late the night before final exams. What were you thinking?
3 Marco may be 30 years old, but he's very _____. He behaves like he's 16!
4 Young-ju works for a Canadian company that plans to _____ ginseng from Korea and China.
5 Before you can use the computer, you need to _____ new software.
6 I thought Cathy's explanation was completely _____. It didn't make any sense to me.
7 Atsushi and his brother are _____. They go everywhere together.

B **Now use *in-*, *il-*, *im-*, or *ir-* to complete the words below. Then, explain the meaning of each word to a partner.**

1 There are still people in the United States who are functionally _____literate—meaning they can hardly read or write.
2 The doctors saved Emilio's life by removing his heart and _____planting an artificial one instead.
3 Here's the list of _____gredients you'll need to make the soup: salt, water, chicken, flour, and onions.
4 Sandra has an _____rational fear of spiders. She's much bigger than they are, after all.
5 During December, the city center was _____luminated by hundreds of colored lights.
6 The government is trying to _____rigate the desert by bringing in water from a river miles away.
7 Cancer is still an _____curable disease.
8 After waiting for Maria for 20 minutes, Albert began to get _____patient.

Chapter 2: Lottery Winners—Rich, but Happy? Unit 4

A Experts have noticed six trends in the recent history of lotteries. Which of these trends seems the most positive to you? Which seem negative? Why?

1 Tickets have become cheaper.
2 The size of grand prizes has increased.
3 Players can choose their own numbers.
4 More different types of lotteries are being introduced.
5 The number of places that sell lottery tickets has increased.
6 The percentage of the money taken in that is paid out has increased.

B Discuss the following questions with a partner.

1 Do you know anyone who has won a lottery or received a lot of money all at one time? What did he or she do with the money?
2 What should a person do right after winning or receiving a lot of money?
3 What bad things can happen to people who win a lottery?

Before You Read:
Lottery Facts

A Take one minute to preview the reading passage. Think about the title and the picture, scan the passage for interesting information, and skim the beginning and ending paragraphs.

B Now discuss these questions about the reading passage with a partner.

1 What do you think the passage is about?
2 Where could you find this kind of an article?
3 What do you already know about this subject?
4 What interesting points did you notice?
5 Do you think you'll enjoy reading the passage?

C Now read through the passage, then answer the questions that follow.

Reading Skill:
Previewing

Previewing is something good readers do when they first encounter new reading material. They ask themselves questions like these: *What is this about? What kind of text is this? What do I already know about it?* Previewing can involve skimming, scanning, and predicting to help us get acquainted with the reading passage.

Lottery Winners— Rich, but Happy?

Every week, millions of dollars are spent, and won, on lottery tickets. The jackpot[1] in many lotteries can be as much as 100 million dollars, and winners suddenly find themselves with more money than ever before. Many will have enough to purchase a new car, build a luxury house, take a holiday, and quit working—all within a short amount of time. The lucky few who hit the jackpot,[2] however, may end up with problems—more than they had before they **struck it rich**. According to Steven Goldbart of a financial planning institute in San Francisco, two out of three winners spend all their winnings within five years.

Lottery winner Michael Carroll

Newly **affluent** lottery winners are actually in quite a tricky situation, and lottery organizers employ counselors to help jackpot winners. These counselors encourage winners to get advice from financial experts, such as accountants,[3] about how best to invest their **windfall**. The counselors also help winners to understand how their lives may change for the better—and possibly for the worse. Luckily, many jackpot winners manage their **fortunes sensibly**. Some winners, however, do not use their money wisely and, as a result, end up getting into various **unforeseen** difficulties.

Case 1

In 2002, 19-year-old English garbage collector Michael Carroll won £10 million in the National Lottery. Three months later, he bought a home in a small town and turned the backyard into a 24-hour racetrack. The constant noise and dust has made his neighbors **irate**. He has purchased several luxury vehicles, and in 2004, Carroll was stopped for driving a brand-new BMW without license plates or insurance, for which he was banned from driving for six years. He has been in frequent trouble with the law due to drugs and other crimes. In 2006 he was jailed for nine months for violent behavior. Upon his release from prison, Carroll applied for loans to make the payments on properties he had bought and to continue his **extravagant** lifestyle. It is reported that his wife and child have left him, and that he is nearly out of money due to overspending on parties, jewelry, cars, houses, etc.

Case 2

In 2005 it was discovered that Laurie Grant of Colchester, Vermont, in the United States was having trouble paying $300 for a driving violation. This was surprising, because ten years before Grant had won a four-million-dollar jackpot. Grant recalled that after she won the lottery she was spending thousands and thousands each day, and that there never seemed to be enough money. She gave an unreported amount of the money away as gifts. Now she finds herself owing the government $270,000. These days, Grant is a part-time factory worker who has a difficult time **keeping up with** her bills. How will she get out of her trouble? Reportedly, Grant believes that she can win the lottery again and plays regularly.

Financial advisors agree that people who win a lottery should follow a few simple rules to secure the future of their fortune. First, meet with an accountant or other financial advisor. Second, pay all debts, such as home mortgages, car loans, and credit card bills. Finally, a winner should calculate how much money he or she will need to live on every year for the rest of his or her life. From that calculation, financial advisors say a person will know exactly how much money should be invested, and how much is left to spend. Only then, advisors suggest, should a lottery winner plan to hand in his or her resignation to the boss.

[40]

¹**jackpot** the biggest or most expensive prize given in a contest
²**hit the jackpot** to win the top prize in a contest
³**accountant** a person who keeps financial records and gives financial advice to a person or company

---

A **How much do you remember from the reading? Choose the best answer for each question below. Try not to look back at the reading for the answers.**

Reading Comprehension:
Check Your Understanding

1 The author of the passage probably wants readers to understand that _____.
   a. winning the lottery solves all of life's problems
   b. winning a huge lottery jackpot may cause as many problems as it solves
   c. even though it brings problems, a huge lottery jackpot is always a good thing

2 How quickly do two out of three lottery winners spend all their winnings?
   a. in one year   **b.** in three years   **c.** in five years

3 What was Michael Carroll's job before he won the lottery?
   a. librarian   **b.** taxi driver   **c.** garbage collector

4 According to the passage, which of the following should lottery winners do first?
   a. talk to a financial advisor
   b. pay all their debts
   c. calculate how much money they need to live for the rest of their life

B **Decide whether the following statements about the reading are true (T) or false (F). If you check (✔) false, correct the statement to make it true.**

	T	F
1 Michael Carroll has spent nearly all of his lottery winnings.		
2 Laurie Grant has a sensible plan about how to get out of trouble.		
3 Michael Carroll has spent time in prison.		
4 Michael Carroll is more generous than Laurie Grant.		

C Critical Thinking

Discuss these questions with a partner.

1 If you won a lot of money, would you handle your money intelligently?
2 What personal qualities help a person to handle money well?
3 Most lottery players don't win very much. Do you think national lotteries are good for these people? Why or why not?

Vocabulary Comprehension:
Words in Context

A **The words in *italics* are vocabulary items from the reading. Read each question or statement and choose the correct answer. Compare your answers with a partner.**

1 An *affluent* person has a lot of _____.
   a. talent   **b.** money
2 If you are *irate*, you are _____ angry.
   a. very   **b.** a little
3 To *keep up with* their work, some people _____.
   a. don't take a vacation   **b.** ask for more work
4 A person with a *fortune* will probably _____.
   a. have to work all of his life   **b.** be able to retire early
5 A *windfall* is a large amount of money that someone _____.
   a. saves for patiently   **b.** receives suddenly
6 An *unforeseen* encounter is a meeting that you _____.
   a. didn't expect   **b.** didn't remember
7 An example of an *extravagant* expense is _____.
   a. a diamond cat collar   **b.** a steam iron
8 A *sensible* person usually _____.
   a. acts without thinking   **b.** thinks before acting
9 My best friend *struck it rich* when he _____.
   a. inherited a cutting-edge computer company from his uncle
   b. got a part-time job at a fashion design firm with a good reputation

B **Answer these questions. Share your answers with a partner.**

1 How did some of the people with the largest *fortunes* originally *strike it rich*?

_____

2 When you feel rich, what is something *extravagant* you like to do?

_____

3 What do some people do when they are *irate*?

_____

4 What are some very sensible ways to use an *unforeseen windfall*?

_____

5 What are some good habits that help you *keep up with* your work and studies?

_____

A Complete each definition below with the correct *-ent* or *-ant* word. Use your dictionary to help you with spelling. Is each word a noun, adjective, or both?

1 a person who lives or resides in a certain place   r_____
2 pleasing to you   p_____
3 when something or someone is unlike another   d_____
4 when something is immediate, quick, very fast   i_____
5 a place where people go to eat a meal   r_____
6 empty, unoccupied   v_____
7 an unfortunate happening, a mishap   a_____
8 a happening or occurrence   e_____

B Think of two more words that end with *-ent* or *-ant*. Write a definition for each and see whether your partner can guess the words.

C Complete the reading below with the correct forms of the *-ent* or *-ant* words from A. You can use the same word more than once.

> Some people become rich by winning the lottery or playing the stock market. Have you ever wondered what it would be like to become a(n) (1)_____ millionaire? Here are some popular urban legends about how people made a lot of money quickly in the United States:
>
> A seventy-nine-year-old New Mexico (2)_____ dropped a cup of coffee she bought from a fast-food (3)_____ on her lap, causing serious burns to her legs and lower body. She sued[1] the (4)_____ for a million dollars and won.
>
> In 1997, a Delaware woman fell from the bathroom window of a popular nightclub. The woman was trying to climb through the window to avoid paying a $3.50 entrance charge. In the (5)_____, she broke her two front teeth. She sued the club for $12,000 and won.
>
> In 1998, a Pennsylvania man was robbing a house. The house was (6)_____ because the owners were away on vacation. The man got locked in the garage and was unable to get out. For eight days, until the (7)_____ returned, the man lived on dog food and soda. He sued the homeowners for $500,000 for his suffering and won.
>
> In 2000, a Texas woman was shopping in a furniture store. She fell over a child who was running around in the store, and broke her ankle. The woman sued the storeowners for $780,000 and won. Here's the strange thing about this (8)_____: the child she fell over was her son.

Vocabulary Skill:
Noun and Adjective Suffixes *-ent* and *-ant*

In this chapter you read the word "affluent," which ends with the suffix "-ent," and "accountant," which ends with the suffix "-ant." These suffixes can both be used to describe someone or something that performs or causes a specific action, e.g., *servant: someone who serves*. The suffixes "-ent" and "-ant" are used with both nouns and adjectives.

---

[1]**sue** to take legal action against someone, usually to get compensation for an injustice

Real Life Skill:
Understanding Money
and Banking Terms

If you're planning a trip to an English-speaking country, especially if you plan to stay for an extended period of time, it is often helpful to learn about money and banking practices. Becoming familiar with some of the local banking customs as well as some of the common money and banking terms will help you to better enjoy your stay.

A The following are common words and phrases used in many English-speaking countries. Discuss their meanings with a partner.

Forms of payment	Using a bank machine	At the bank
cash	ATM*	open a checking account
check	PIN**	currency exchange
debit card	withdraw	money transfer
credit card	deposit	
	balance	
	receipt	

*Automated Teller Machine   **Personal Identification Number

B Complete the information below using words and phrases from the chart in A.

1 In many countries, you might use a _____ to reserve a hotel room.
2 You want to send or receive money electronically. You should visit a bank or a credit agency and ask about _____.
3 You have money from your country, but you need American dollars. You should visit a place that does _____.
4 You have $500 in your checking account. You go to the ATM and _____ $85. What is your _____ now?

C Below is a common form of payment in the United States. What is it? Imagine you need to pay $55.35 to Kean's Department Store. Complete the missing information.

222 Shannon Street,   811
San Francisco, CA 94134   Date _____

Pay to the order of _____ $ [   ]
_____ DOLLARS

Bank of America
1234 001 234 567   _____

What Do You Think?

1 Do you think you will be rich someday? How will you feel if you're not?
2 There is a saying, "Money cannot buy happiness." Do you agree or disagree? Explain your answer.
3 Can you name any millionaires or billionaires in the world? What about in your country? What do they do?
4 What project or organization do you think is most worthy of receiving a million-dollar donation?

Getting Ready

Discuss the following questions with a partner.

1 Describe what you see in each of the photos above.
2 What cultural events (weddings, birthdays, holidays, etc.) are each of the photos related to?
  Try to think of as many as you can for each photo.
3 When did you last personally experience the things shown in the photos?
4 What is your favorite cultural event or custom? Explain your answer.

Chapter 1: Wedding Customs

A **How much do you know about weddings? Answer these questions, then check your answers with a partner.**

1 The word *bride* comes from the Old English word for _____.
   a. wife   **b.** love   **c.** cook
2 A man traditionally proposes to a woman _____.
   a. on both knees   **b.** on one knee   **c.** standing up
3 The best man custom began in Germany. He originally helped the groom _____.
   a. get dressed   **b.** choose a bride   **c.** capture his bride from another village
4 What is the color of a traditional wedding gown?
   a. red   **b.** green   **c.** white
5 Which of these expressions means "to get married"?
   a. tie the knot   **b.** kick the bucket   **c.** buy the farm

B **Discuss the following questions with a partner.**

1 At what age do men and women in your country usually get married?
2 What are some popular wedding customs?
3 In what ways have weddings changed over the years?

A **Skim the reading passage quickly. Notice the title, subheads, photos, and any other interesting information.**

B **What is this reading mainly about?**

1 how to include the best wedding customs in your wedding
2 the meaning and origin of wedding customs
3 why some wedding customs are confusing

C **Read through the passage again, then answer the questions that follow.**

Skimming is one way to look for the main ideas in a reading. When we skim, we read over parts of the text very quickly. We don't need to read every word, or look up words we don't understand; we just need to get a general idea of what the passage is about.

Wedding Customs

Marriage is an ancient religious and legal practice celebrated around the world. Although the reasons that people marry are similar in many places, wedding customs vary from country to country.

The Wedding Dress

In many countries, it is customary for the bride to wear a white dress as
5 a symbol of **purity**. The tradition of wearing a special white dress only
for the wedding ceremony started around 150 years ago. Before that,
most women could not afford to buy a dress that they would only wear
once. Now, bridal dresses can be bought in a variety of styles and **fabrics**,
and many brides have their dress specially made. In some countries, colors
10 other than white are worn by the bride or used as part of the wedding
ceremony. In certain Asian countries and in the Middle East, red and
orange are considered symbols of joy and happiness. In Asia it is not
uncommon for the bride and groom to change clothes more than once
as the ceremony **progresses**.

The Wedding Veil

15 As part of many traditional wedding ceremonies, a bride wears a veil. Wearing a veil that covers the
head and face is a tradition that is over 2,000 years old. Veils were originally worn as a sign of secrecy
and **modesty** and could only be removed by the husband after the ceremony. Today, many brides wear
a veil, but only for decoration. In some countries, a veil is placed between the bride and groom during
20 the wedding ceremony so that they cannot see or touch each other until they are married.

The Rings

In many cultures, couples exchange rings, usually made of gold or silver,
during the marriage ceremony. The circular shape of the ring is symbolic
of the couple's **eternal union**. In Brazil, it is traditional to have the rings
25 **engraved**, with the bride's name on the groom's ring, and vice versa.[1]
The wedding ring is usually worn on the third finger of the left or right
hand, because it was once believed that a vein[2] ran directly from this
finger to the heart.

Flowers

30 Flowers play an important role in most weddings. Roses are said to be the flowers of love, and because
roses usually **bloom** in June, this has become the most popular month for weddings in many countries.
Ivy is also used in wedding bouquets[3] because in early Greek times it was thought to be a sign of
everlasting love. After the wedding ceremony, it is customary in many countries for the bride to throw
her bouquet into a crowd of well wishers—usually her single female friends. It is said that the person
35 who catches the bouquet will be the next one to marry.

Gifts

In Chinese cultures, wedding guests give gifts of money to the newlyweds in small red envelopes. Money is also an appropriate gift at Korean and Japanese weddings. Not all cultures, however, consider money an appropriate gift. In many Western countries, for example in the U.K., wedding guests give the bride and
40 groom household items that they may need for their new home. In Russia, rather than receiving gifts, the bride and groom provide gifts to their guests instead. In Scotland, a week before the wedding ceremony, the bride's mother may invite the guests to her house and **show off** all the wedding gifts received, unwrapped, each with a card that has the giver's name on it.

With the continued internationalization of the modern world, wedding customs that originated in one
45 part of the world are crossing national boundaries and have been incorporated into marriage ceremonies in other countries. Couples frequently use a variety of traditional customs from different cultures in creating a memorable wedding ceremony.

---

[1]**vice versa** the same, but also in reverse; the opposite is also true
[2]**vein** a small tube in the body that carries blood to the heart
[3]**bouquet** a group of flowers put together, usually to be given as a gift or to be held in a ceremony

---

Reading Comprehension:
Check Your Understanding

A How much do you remember from the reading? Choose the best answer to complete each statement below.

1 The tradition of wearing a special dress only on one's wedding day is about _____ years old.
   a. 150   **b.** 2,000   **c.** 2,500

2 In some cultures, the bride wears a white dress as a traditional symbol of _____.
   a. modesty   **b.** purity   **c.** secrecy

3 In some Asian and Middle Eastern countries, which color is NOT considered to be a happy color for a wedding?
   a. red   **b.** orange   **c.** blue

4 According to the reading, in which country would the wedding guests give the bride and groom money?
   a. Brazil   **b.** the U.K.   **c.** China

B Complete the sentences with information from the reading. Write no more than three words for each answer.

1 In many cultures, a wedding ring is worn on the third finger because people believed this finger was connected _____.

2 There is a belief that the person who catches the bride's bouquet will be the next _____.

3 It is customary to engrave the bride and groom's names on wedding rings in _____.

4 In Scotland, the bride's mother may invite the wedding guests to her house in order to show off the _____.

C Critical Thinking

Discuss these questions with a partner.

1 Which of the customs from the reading would you like to include in your own wedding celebrations?
2 How much is a reasonable amount of money to spend on a wedding?
3 What are some good gifts for newly married couples?

A For each group, circle the word that does not belong. The words in *italics* are vocabulary items from the reading.

1 *bloom*	encounter	meet	bump into
2 written	*engraved*	printed	conducted
3 everlasting	ultimate	*eternal*	unending
4 soar	fly	climb	*fabric*
5 *modesty*	supply	shyness	reserve
6 advance	*progress*	revive	continue
7 cleanliness	spotlessness	*purity*	awareness
8 hide	conceal	cover	*show off*
9 *union*	connection	era	oneness

B Complete the sentences using the words in *italics* from A. Be sure to use the correct form of the word.

1 White flowers are a symbol of _____.
2 As the procession _____ down the street in front of us, we waved to the people.
3 Eileen loves to _____ her engagement ring to her jealous friends.
4 A wedding ring is a symbol of the _____ between two people that is _____ and will never end.
5 The jeweler _____ the wrong name inside my wedding ring.
6 The _____ used to make this tent is unusually dense. Water will never come through it.
7 In the spring, flowers _____ and show us their beautiful colors.
8 Because of her _____, Sarah would never speak out during class discussions, even if she had good ideas.

Vocabulary Skill:

Word Families

When you learn a new word in English, it is helpful to also learn words that are related to it. Learning the different parts of speech that form the word family can help you to expand your vocabulary.

A Complete the chart with the noun, verb, and adjective forms of words you've seen in this chapter. Be careful—not every word will have all three. Look again at the reading to find related words, or use your dictionary to help you.

Noun	Verb	Adjective
symbol		
		decorative
custom		
	progress	
purity		
		traditional
		eternal

B Now complete the paragraph below with the correct word from the chart. Be sure to use the correct form of the word.

Wedding Symbols and Superstitions

What will bring good luck to the bride and groom on their wedding day? Different cultures have different beliefs, but nearly all do something to wish the couple a long and happy marriage.

In Italy, it's (1)_____ for the wedding guests to tie a ribbon in front of the building where the couple will marry. This is a (2)_____ of the couple's (3)_____ bond of marriage. There is another (4)_____ in which the bride gives guests "confetti," which are small bags of candy-covered almonds. Confetti is a (5)_____ of fertility or the ability to have children.

In Korea, ducks and geese (6)_____ faithfulness because they stay together for life. Many years ago, when a man found a wife, he would often give her family a pair of geese. Today, a Korean wedding ceremony may include (7)_____ such as hand-painted ducks. These are a (8)_____ of the couple's promise to stay together.

In Japan, in addition to wearing a white kimono, many women were traditionally painted completely white. This was done as a sign that the woman was (9)_____. The woman also wore a heavy headpiece. On this were many beautiful (10)_____. People believed this headpiece could attract good luck to the couple.

Chapter 2: That Unique Japanese Holiday Called . . . Christmas!

A Match the traditions on the left with their holidays on the right.

1 eating turkey _____
2 giving gifts of chocolate _____
3 dressing up in frightening costumes _____
4 decorating a tree in one's home _____
5 a party that goes past midnight _____

a. Halloween
b. New Year's Eve
c. Christmas
d. Thanksgiving Day
e. Saint Valentine's Day

B Discuss the following questions with a partner.

1 Do you have a favorite holiday? Which one is it?
2 What holiday traditions are unique to your country?
3 Has your culture borrowed any traditions from other countries?

A Take one minute to preview the reading passage. Think about the title and the picture, scan the passage for interesting information, and skim the beginning and ending paragraphs. Then decide if the following statements are true (T) or false (F).

Reading Skill:
Predicting

		T	F
1	Christmas is a holiday that is celebrated in Japan.		
2	Christmas is celebrated the same way in Japan as in Western countries.		
3	Nobody works on Christmas Day in Japan.		
4	Ten percent of the Japanese population is Christian.		
5	It's common for the Japanese to adapt foreign customs and make them their own.		

Good readers naturally make predictions before they begin to read. Making predictions starts us thinking about the text, and it also activates the knowledge we may already have about the topic. As a result, we're more ready to continue reading once we start.

B Skim the passage to check whether your predictions in A are correct, and discuss your answers with a partner.

C Read through the passage, then answer the questions that follow.

That Unique Japanese Holiday Called . . . Christmas!

People in Western countries are often surprised to learn that the Japanese celebrate Christmas. To the Westerner who visits Japan at the end of the year, many sights and sounds are familiar: the Santas in the **media** ads, the big displays and the Christmas music in the stores, the lights on the houses, the decorated trees within.

Learn more about how the Japanese celebrate the end-of-year holidays, however, and you begin to realize that the Japanese **interpretation** of Christmas is something rather different. For one thing, Christmas is more of a fun beginning to the holidays rather than the main event. In Japan, the most important holiday of the season is New Year's Day, which comes one week later. New Year is the big traditional holiday when family and friends get together. In fact, Christmas is not officially a holiday at all—most people have to work that day unless it happens to fall on a weekend. As a result, people celebrate on Christmas Eve.

What do the Japanese do on Christmas Eve? Often they go out for dinner at a fancy restaurant. This custom has become very popular, and most good restaurants sell out for that evening. Because so many couples go out on that night, Christmas has become **associated** with romance, rather like Saint Valentine's Day in the West. It is the ideal time for people in love to go out for a special, romantic evening. They dress up, give each other presents, and enjoy a delicious meal.

The food is an important part of the Christmas celebrations. Japanese do not usually eat roast turkey or baked ham on Christmas. They are more likely to eat fried or roast teriyaki chicken, fried potatoes, cheese-stuffed wonton, or even pizza. The favorite dessert is "Christmas cake." Christmas cake is something that hardly exists in the West. It is a light, not very sweet cake covered with whipped cream and fruit such as strawberries, with possibly a plastic Santa Claus for decoration on top. Stores everywhere compete to sell their distinctive **versions** of Christmas cake before the holiday and then lower the price dramatically on December 25.

As in the West, gift-giving is a big part of the holiday, but it takes on its own character in Japan. On their big night out, romantic partners may give each other flowers, cute toys, or rings or other jewelry. Within the family, parents may give presents to their young children, but children do not usually give

anything to their parents. The idea here is that the gifts come from Santa Claus, so it only makes sense
to give them while the children are still young enough to believe in Santa. And there are the presents,
35 called *oseibo*, which are given between companies, to the boss, to teachers or other people outside
the immediate circle of family or friends. These gifts are part of the Japanese tradition of showing
appreciation to people who have performed some type of service for you.

It is not really surprising that the Japanese have interpreted Christmas in their own fashion. Christians
make up only a very small part (less than 2%) of the population, so people are not very familiar with the
40 religious roots of the holiday. In addition, over the centuries the Japanese have shown an amazing ability
for importing **institutions** from other cultures and adapting them to their own needs. For example,
Buddhism, the **parliamentary** form of government, large **corporations**, and the current educational
system all came originally from abroad. It may be that these institutions are so successful in today's
Japan because they are no longer exactly the same as they were. In the process of **adopting** them, the
45 Japanese made them uniquely their own.

Reading Comprehension: Check Your Understanding

A Decide whether the following statements about the reading are true (T) or false (F). If you check (✔) false, correct the statement to make it true.

		T	F
1	This passage is about mistakes Japanese make celebrating Christmas.		
2	Japanese people go out to dinner at a fancy restaurant on Christmas Day.		
3	In Japan, Christmas is thought of as a romantic holiday.		
4	Many young people in Japan believe that Santa Claus is real.		
5	Japan's current educational system was developed in Japan.		

B Complete the sentences about the reading with the correct information, then discuss your answers with a partner.

1 The most important holiday for the Japanese at the end of the year is _____.

2 Christmas cakes are sometimes decorated with a plastic _____ on top.

3 Gifts exchanged between companies at the end of the year are called _____.

4 Buddhism and Japan's form of government came to Japan _____.

C Critical Thinking

Discuss these questions with a partner.

1 Do you think the author considers the Japanese way of celebrating Christmas to be incorrect? Why or why not?
2 Why does the author point out that the Japanese do not eat roast turkey or baked ham on Christmas?

Vocabulary Comprehension:
Word Definitions

A Look at the list of words and phrases from the reading. Match each with a definition on the right.

1 adopt _____
2 associated _____
3 appreciation _____
4 institution _____
5 interpret _____
6 media _____
7 parliament _____
8 corporation _____
9 version _____

a. television, radio, magazines, the Internet, etc.
b. to find the meaning of something
c. a form of something that is slightly different from other forms of the same thing
d. a group of elected people who make a country's laws
e. connected
f. thanks
g. a custom or tradition that has existed for a long time
h. to accept or start to use something new
i. company; business

B Complete the sentences below using the words from A. Be sure to use the correct form of the word.

1 Many _____ move their head offices to other countries to reduce the amount of tax they must pay.
2 Our company _____ a cutting-edge computer system last week.
3 I bought a gift to show my friend how much I _____ her help.
4 The _____ is a governmental _____ that is an important part of many modern democracies.
5 The _____ broadcast two different _____ of the news story, which confused the viewers.
6 The soaring cost of living is _____ with the rising price of oil.
7 For years scientists have tried to _____ the meaning of whale songs.

A Match the words on the left with their definitions on the right. You can use your dictionary to help you.

Vocabulary Skill:
Homophones

Homophones

1 adds _____
2 adze _____
3 isle _____
4 aisle _____
5 overdue _____
6 overdo _____
7 band _____
8 banned _____
9 sore_____
10 soar _____

Definitions

a. forbidden; prohibited
b. to do too much of something
c. the short form of island
d. a tool for shaping wood
e. performs addition
f. to fly high
g. a corridor or space between rows of chairs
h. a music group
i. painful
j. past the time of payment

In this unit you read the word "sights." This word, however, sounds exactly the same as the word "sites" to our ear, although it is spelled slightly differently. Words like these are called "homophones," and there are many such words in English.

B Complete the sentences below using the homophones from A.

1 Noisy airplanes _____ over my house every day because I live near the airport.

2 John is really good at calculation. He _____ numbers faster than anyone I know.

3 My wife is irate because I forgot to pay the rent, and now it's _____.

4 I've been writing for so long that my hand is _____.

5 When I fly in airplanes, I like to sit by the _____ and not the window.

6 I hope to realize my dream one day of playing guitar in a rock _____.

7 I never work out at the gym for more than one hour. I don't want to _____ it.

8 From the ship, through the dense fog, we could see a small _____ covered with trees in the middle of the ocean.

9 I was hoping to make some furniture, but I cannot find my _____.

10 In an attempt to stop inflation, price increases have been _____.

Real Life Skill:
Accepting and Declining Invitations

People often send invitations by regular post or e-mail asking others to join them for a meal, a celebratory party, or a night out. Some words and phrases are typically found in invitations. Certain expressions are also used to accept or decline an invitation.

A Look at the highlighted words in the invitation below. What do you think they mean?

> You're **invited** to Tom and Amy's **engagement party**!
>
> **The Blue Moon**
> 1453 South Mission Boulevard
>
> Saturday, May 17, 7:00 P.M. – **late**
> **Cocktails** and **hors d'oeuvres** will be served.
> **Dress code**: Casual
> **RSVP**: No later than May 1

B Read the two replies. Who is going to the party? Who isn't? Underline the words and phrases that helped you decide.

> May 1
> Tom and Amy,
> Thanks for the invitation; the party sounds like a lot of fun. I'm afraid I won't be able to make it, though. I'm going to be out of town that weekend. Congratulations on the marriage plans!
> Toshi

> April 25
> Tom and Amy,
> Thanks for the invitation; the party sounds like a lot of fun. Kim and I are coming. Looking forward to seeing you!
> Rita

C You are invited to Tom and Amy's party. Using the expressions you've learned, send a reply accepting or declining the invitation.

What Do You Think?

1 Describe your ideal wedding. What would it be like? Whom would you invite? Where would it take place?

2 Have there been any interesting celebrity weddings lately? Which ones caught your attention?

3 Japan does not only adopt things from abroad. In what ways has Japan influenced the world?

4 If you could go anywhere in the world on any holiday, which place and which holiday would you choose? Explain your answer.

It's a Mystery

Unit 6

Getting Ready

Discuss the following questions with a partner.

1 Look at the photos above. Do you know where these things are?
2 Do you know of any theories about how or why these things were made?
3 What other mysterious structures or places on Earth do you know?
4 Do you think there are some things that cannot be explained by science? If so, what are some examples?

Unit 6 — Chapter 1: Mystery Tours

Before You Read:
Famous Enigmas

A Where in the world are these three mysterious structures? Scan the reading passage, then match each with a location.

Structure
1 the moai _____
2 Stonehenge _____
3 the Nazca lines _____

Location
a. Peru
b. the South Pacific
c. England

B Discuss the following questions with a partner.

1 Would you like to take a trip to a faraway and mysterious place? Why or why not?
2 Who do you think created the moai? Stonehenge? The Nazca lines?
3 What do you think are the purposes of these three mysterious structures?

Reading Skill:
Identifying Fact Versus Theory

When we read we are often presented with *facts*, but we may also encounter *theories* that are not proven. Facts are accepted as true, while theories may or may not be true. Knowing the difference will help us correctly understand what we read.

A Read these pieces of information from the reading. Write F if you think the information is a fact, and T if you think it is a theory.

The Moai of Easter Island
1 The moai are religious symbols. _____
2 There are about 600 moai. _____

Stonehenge
3 Stonehenge was built to be an ancient temple. _____
4 Stonehenge was built without heavy-lifting equipment. _____

The Nazca Lines
5 The Nazca lines are etched into the earth. _____
6 The Nazca lines are related to religious beliefs. _____

B Skim the passage to find out whether your answers in A are correct. Check your answers with a partner.

C Read through the passage again, then answer the questions that follow.

Mystery Tours

Travel with us to mysterious locations that still **baffle** archeologists to this day. We offer tours to three spectacular locations: Easter Island in the South Pacific, Stonehenge in England, and the Nazca Desert of Peru. These places hold extraordinarily impressive, ancient structures created by prehistoric civilizations. Scientists can only **speculate** as to how they were made. Take this
5 opportunity to experience these mysteries in person!

The Moai of Easter Island

Located in the South Pacific, Easter Island is one of the most **isolated** places on Earth and is famous for the large stone statues that
10 line its coast. These **intriguing** statues, which were carved by ancient people to **resemble** human heads, range in height from about 3½ to 12 meters. Today, roughly 600 of the statues, called moai, are still standing.

15 Archeological research suggests that Easter Island was first inhabited by Polynesians[1] around A.D. 400. Scientists believe these early inhabitants carved the island's moai— believed to be religious symbols—from
20 volcanic rock, and then pulled them to their different locations.

Stonehenge

On the opposite side of the world stands Stonehenge. This ancient English site is a collection of large stones arranged in two circles—one inside the other. Although only ruins of the original
25 formation exist today, archaeologists believe that the inner circle of bluestones, each weighing about four tons, was built first. The giant stones that form the outer circle, known as sarsen stones, each weigh as much as 50 tons!

Exactly how and why Stonehenge was constructed remains a mystery. Research suggests that it may have been designed and built by an ancient religious group who used it for one of two purposes;
30 either as a sacred temple or as an observatory to study the sky. Scientists believe that the enormous stones were transported from places around the country—some up to 240 miles away—to their present site on Salisbury Plain in southern England. Work on the monument is thought to have started around 2000 B.C. and continued to 1500 B.C. Today, engineers estimate that approximately 600 people were needed to transport each sarsen stone from its point of origin to Salisbury.
35 Scientists consider this a remarkable feat, given that heavy lifting equipment used in modern construction was not available at that time.

The Nazca Lines

In South America, another mysterious **phenomenon** exists. Near the coast of Peru, on the high plateau of the Nazca Desert, some remarkable art is etched[2] into the earth. Viewed from the ground, these
40 etchings seem **insignificant**. Viewed from high above, however, these large drawings on the Earth's surface resemble birds, fish, seashells, and geometric[3] shapes. These drawings are thought to be at least 1,500 years old, yet have remained preserved for centuries by the dry, stable climate of the desert.

Many theories exist about the ancient peoples of the Nazca Desert and their purposes for creating these mysterious lines.

45 Some scientists suggest that the lines at Nazca are related to the religious beliefs of an ancient civilization. These people believed that the mountain gods protected them by controlling the weather and the supply of water. Many of the figures formed by the lines are associated with nature or water in some way. As the ancient people lived in a desert region, water was a valuable but scarce resource. Exactly how the lines were drawn without the help of aerial[4] monitoring equipment, though, remains an
50 **enigma**.

Awaken your inner explorer and sign up now for one of our unforgettable mystery tours. The incredible sensation of **witnessing** first-hand these prehistoric marvels defies description. You simply have to experience it for yourself.

[1]**Polynesians** native people of the South Pacific islands between Hawaii, New Zealand, and Easter Island
[2]**etch** to make a picture by cutting lines into a hard surface such as metal, wood, or stone
[3]**geometric** having simple, regular lines or forms
[4]**aerial** above ground; in the air

Reading Comprehension:
Check Your Understanding

A Decide whether the following statements about the reading are true (T) or false (F). If you check (✔) false, correct the statement to make it true.

	T	F
1 The reading talks about three places that have puzzled scientists for years.		
2 Drawings in the Nazca Desert look like animals and seashells from the ground.		
3 It is believed the structures on Easter Island were carved from volcanic rock.		
4 Scientists know how the drawings in the Nazca Desert were made.		
5 It probably took about 500 years to build Stonehenge.		

B Are these statements about the moai of Easter Island, Stonehenge, or the Nazca lines? Write M, S, or N.

1 There are two rings of large stones, one inside the other. _____
2 Some of them look like birds. _____

3 The dry climate has preserved them. _____
4 They are 3½ to 12 meters in height. _____

C Critical Thinking

Discuss these questions with a partner.

1 Why would a company offer tours to these places?
2 What other mysterious places might attract tourists?
3 Do you think we will solve these mysteries in the future?

A **The words in *italics* are vocabulary items from the reading. Read each question or statement and choose the correct answer. Check your answers with a partner.**

Vocabulary Comprehension:
Words in Context

1 A person will most likely *resemble* his or her _____.
   a. mother or father   **b.** husband or wife
2 An *isolated* place is probably _____.
   a. mysterious   **b.** hard to get to
3 Which of the following is an *enigma*?
   a. How are children born?   **b.** Is there life after death?
4 If you *witness* a crime, you _____.
   a. hear about it from someone   **b.** see it with your own eyes
5 A *baffling* illness is _____ for doctors to treat.
   a. easy   **b.** difficult
6 Which question might most people find *intriguing*?
   a. How many planets are there in our solar system?
   b. Is there intelligent life on other planets?
7 Which might be considered an unusual *phenomenon*?
   a. a robot vacuum cleaner   **b.** a snowstorm in summer
8 If people *speculate* that the price of oil will rise, they _____.
   a. think it might rise   **b.** are sure it will rise
9 You are applying for a visa to enter the United States. Which information is *insignificant*?
   a. your age   **b.** your favorite color

B **Answer these questions. Discuss your answers with a partner.**

1 Whom do people say that you *resemble*?
2 Name two remarkable *phenomena*—one natural and one man-made.
3 Give an example of an *isolated* locale.
4 What important event have you *witnessed*?
5 In your opinion, what is the most *intriguing enigma* of life?
6 What things do you *speculate* will be more expensive next year?

Vocabulary Skill:

The Root Word
spec + Prefixes

In this unit you learned the word "speculation," meaning "guessing about something." This word begins with the root word "spec," meaning "to observe" or "to watch," and is combined with the noun suffix "-tion," meaning "the act of." This root (sometimes also written "spic") is combined with prefixes and suffixes to form many words in English. When it is used with some prefixes such as "ex-," the spelling of the word changes.

A Here are some common prefixes used with the root *spec*. Match the prefix with its correct meaning.

1 ex-   a. below, under
2 in-   b. forward
3 intro-   c. out, away
4 pro-   d. back, backward
5 retro-   e. within
6 sub-   f. into

B Look at the words below. What do you think they mean? What part of speech is each? Complete the sentences below with the correct word.

> expect   suspect   inspect
> prospective   introspective   retrospect

1 The police _____ Angela stole the money, but they can't prove it.
2 We _____ the plane will arrive on time; it's scheduled to come in at 3:00 this afternoon.
3 Ricardo got married at age 20, but in _____, he thinks he should have waited until he was older.
4 Carmen has two _____ buyers for her paintings. She feels certain that at least one will purchase some of her work.
5 Celine is a rather quiet and _____ young woman.
6 When I arrived in London, the customs officials opened my bags to _____ the contents.

C Think of two more words using *spec*. Write a sentence for each. Use your dictionary to help you.

1 _____
_____
2 _____
_____

Chapter 2: Is "Spontaneous Human Combustion" Possible?

A Discuss the following questions with a partner.

1 Do you think that science can explain everything that happens in the world? Why or why not?
2 Can you think of any unusual events that people cannot explain?
3 Are you quick to believe in mysteries, or do you need to be shown proof before you will believe in things?

B Read the following claims. Which do you think are true? Which do you think are false?

	T	F
1 Some people are able to move things using their minds.		
2 Some people have died by mysteriously catching fire, although there was no source of fire near them at the time.		
3 Earth is frequently visited by beings from other worlds.		
4 If you talk to your plants and play soft music for them, they grow better.		

A Read the sentences below. Which sentence best helps you to understand the meaning of the word *ventilated*? Explain your answer to a partner.

1 This room is well ventilated.
2 This room is well ventilated because it has lots of windows.
3 This room is well ventilated because it has lots of windows so air can pass through easily.

B Find each italicized word in the reading below. Read the sentence in which the word appears and some of the surrounding sentences. Then choose the best definition.

1 In the reading title, the word *spontaneous* probably means _____.
   a. unstoppable   **b.** sudden   **c.** frightening
2 In the reading title, the word *combustion* probably means _____.
   a. burning   **b.** action   **c.** combination
3 In line 29, the word *function* probably means _____.
   a. work   **b.** burn   **c.** change
4 In line 33, the word *external* probably means _____.
   a. from behind   **b.** from above   **c.** from outside

> To guess the meaning of an important but unfamiliar word in a reading passage, try the following: First, think about how the new word is related to the topic of the reading. Second, identify what part of speech the word is. Third, look at the words surrounding the new word for synonyms, antonyms, or an explanation of the word.

Is "Spontaneous Human Combustion" Possible?

It happens something like this. Someone finds a badly burnt body in a poorly **ventilated** room. The body is sitting in a chair or lying on a bed or the floor. The upper body of the **victim** is a heap of ashes, but one or
5　more mostly undamaged hands or feet may be visible as well. A layer of blackened grease covers the ceiling and walls above the victim's head, but fire damage in the room is limited to a small area right around and above the body. Objects only a few feet away remain
10　untouched by the blaze. Police investigators find no obvious source or cause for the fire.

This scene describes a typical case of **spontaneous** human combustion (SHC), in which a human body is **supposedly** able to burst into flames and to burn to almost nothing entirely on its own. In most SHC cases there are no witnesses to see how the person caught fire. However, sometimes there are. In
15　a few cases the observer, who is often a friend or family member, sees the person burst into flame and tries to **put out** the fire. Occasionally the victim survives. Again, there is no clear outside cause—the blaze appears to start from within the victim's own body.

This phenomenon is actually nothing new. A 1763 book by Frenchman Jonas Dupont with the title *De Incendiis Corporis Humani Spontaneis* describes in detail a number of cases of SHC. A century
20　later Charles Dickens used SHC to kill off one of the characters in his novel *Bleak House*. A number of more recent unexplained deaths have helped to keep the theory of SHC alive. An example is that of Agnes Phillips, who burned to death in Sydney, Australia, in 1991. Phillips' daughter had left her sleeping in a car near a shopping center for a few minutes when she saw smoke. A thorough investigation revealed no source for the blaze. The car's engine had been turned off and there were no
25　cigarettes in the vehicle.

People have tried to explain these mysterious deaths in various ways. Some have said that SHC can be set off by a build-up of electricity or of gases within the body. The most reasonable explanation seems to be the "wick" or "candle" theory. This says that under certain circumstances the human body can **function** as sort of an **inside-out** candle. That is, the fabric in a person's clothing acts like the wick
30　and the fat in a person's body like the wax in the candle. The burning clothes cause a person's body fat to melt, adding fuel to the fire. In a poorly ventilated room the body can burn for hours and cause the kind of damage seen in many of the supposed SHC cases. In this scenario the combustion is not "spontaneous" at all, and is always caused by some **external** fire source.

In a recent experiment, the criminologist Dr. John de Haan put the wick theory to the test. De Haan

35 wrapped a dead pig (chosen because the body fat of a pig is similar to that of a human) in a blanket, poured gasoline over it, set it on fire and then let it burn in a badly ventilated room. After burning for several hours, the body of the pig was reduced to ashes, much like the bodies of many supposed SHC victims.

40 De Haan's experiment did not persuade everyone that the wick theory explains SHC. Some believe there are still too many unanswered questions in many of the cases. What about the situations where no external source of the fire was found or where victims have **burst into flame** in front of witnesses? Until scientists come up with a theory that explains all of these circumstances, many will likely continue to believe in the possibility of spontaneous human combustion.

A **How much do you remember from the reading? Read each question or statement below and choose the correct answer.**

1 The author probably wrote this article in order to _____.
 a. convince people that spontaneous human combustion is true
 b. warn people that spontaneous human combustion can happen to them
 c. explain and tell the history of spontaneous human combustion
2 Who used the idea of SHC to kill off a fictional character?
 a. Jonas Dupont **b.** Charles Dickens **c.** Dr. John de Haan
3 According to the "wick" theory, what fuels an SHC fire?
 a. body fat **b.** electricity **c.** gases
4 In a true case of SHC, the fire source would need to be _____.
 a. external **b.** a cigarette **c.** internal

B **Decide whether the following statements about the reading are true (T) or false (F), or whether the information is not given (NG). If you check (✔) false, correct the statement to make it true.**

	T	F	NG
1 Victims of spontaneous human combustion always die.			
2 Spontaneous human combustion usually happens to old people.			
3 John de Haan tested the "wick" theory with an experiment.			
4 Everyone believes in John de Haan's theory of SHC.			

C Critical Thinking

Discuss these questions with a partner.

1 Do you believe in spontaneous human combustion? Why or why not?

2 Is there any way to prove whether SHC is actually true?

Vocabulary Comprehension:
Odd Word Out

A For each group, (circle) the word that does not belong. The words in *italics* are vocabulary items from the reading.

1	*burst into flame*	catch fire	make a statement	start burning
2	extravagant	*external*	outer	exterior
3	show off	boast	*function*	brag
4	upside-down	reversed	fitting	*inside-out*
5	*put out*	douse	extinguish	conduct
6	eternal	*spontaneous*	unplanned	sudden
7	possibly	intentionally	*supposedly*	apparently
8	bloom	air out	aerate	*ventilate*
9	*victim*	signal	cue	sign

B Complete the sentences below using the words in *italics* from A. Be sure to use the correct form of the word.

1 James Bond has a custom-made watch that also _____ as a compass.

2 Gina has a reputation for being _____. She does what she wants, when she wants, without warning.

3 During the race, the car's engine _____, but the driver escaped unharmed.

4 When painting the interior of a house, make sure the area is well _____.

5 This jacket is green on one side, but black if you turn it _____.

6 The _____ of the attack told a different version of the story than his attacker.

7 _____, a man in London has witnessed a case of SHC, but I don't believe it.

8 I'll have to ask you to _____ your cigarette before boarding the train.

9 The _____ part of the space shuttle gets very hot as it travels down to earth.

A Look at the examples below.

1 Verb + Preposition
Some verbs can be used with certain prepositions.
*My big dictionary also **functions as** a doorstop.*
*Jane's parents **regarded** her announcement of marriage **with** surprise.*

2 Adjective + Noun
Certain noun and adjective combinations work together to talk about one thing.
*Let's get some **fresh air**.*
*He is my **close / good / best friend**.*

3 Verb + Noun
Some nouns go with certain verbs to talk about one idea.
*Who is going to **make dinner**?*
*When will you **go shopping**?*

B Look at the words in the box below. What part of speech is each one? Match them with the nouns and prepositions to form some common word combinations. Some words will have more than one match. Use your dictionary to help you. Compare your ideas with a partner.

> make   do   go   hard   short
> think   move   hope   know   work

1 _____ a decision
2 _____ with
3 _____ for
4 _____ about
5 _____ time
6 _____ for
7 _____ as
8 _____ of
9 _____ to
10 _____ work

C Complete the paragraph below with the correct noun, verb, adjective, or preposition. Be sure to use the correct form of the word. Check your answers with a partner.

Not many people know (1) _____ Alfred R. Riddle, the mystery hunter. When Alfred was very young, he (2) _____ a decision to dedicate his life to hunting mysteries. When he finished college, he moved (3) _____ Scotland for a (4) _____ time to look for the Loch Ness Monster. Later, he worked (5) _____ the U.S. government, observing the skies for UFOs. After that, he went (6) _____ Nepal, where he hoped (7) _____ discover the Yeti. He had a very (8) _____ time finding anything in all that snow, and Alfred never really liked (9) _____ work. Alfred decided to give up mystery hunting and now spends most of his time watching mystery programs on television.

Real Life Skill:
Researching Mysteries Online

The Internet contains a wealth of information about mysteries. Searching the Internet is an important skill. The Internet has a lot of useful and interesting information. Even if you can't understand all the writing on a website, your scanning skills can guide you to the information you want.

A Look at this list of mysterious places. Choose three you would like to research online, or use your own ideas.

> The Great Pyramid   The Sphinx   Baalbeck   Bermuda Triangle
> Fatima   Atlantis   Machu Picchu   Chichen Itza   Kailasa Temple

B Search the Internet for information about the three mysterious places you chose in A. Complete the chart with the location and information about the place.

	Location and Other Information
Mysterious Place 1	
Mysterious Place 2	
Mysterious Place 3	

C Share the information you found with a partner.

What Do You Think?

1 Which of the mysteries you learned about in this unit is most intriguing to you? Why?
2 Do you know any mysteries that have been proven to be false? Which ones?
3 What would the world be like if there weren't any mysteries in it?

Fluency Strategy: *KWL*

Readers can ask themselves three questions to improve their reading fluency and comprehension. The letters K, W, and L can be used to remind you of these questions. KWL stands for **K**now, **W**ant, **L**earn.

Know

The first step of KWL is similar to the Survey stage in SQ3R (page 139) and the A in the ACTIVE approach (inside front cover). This step will help you prepare yourself before reading.

A Look at the title of the article on the next page. Then read only the first paragraph of the passage. From the title and first paragraph, decide, "What is the topic of the passage?"

B Ask yourself, "What do I already know about this topic?" Write down three or four facts that you already know about the topic in the Know column of the table below.

Know	Want	Learn
1 _____ _____	1 _____ _____	1 _____ _____
2 _____ _____	2 _____ _____	2 _____ _____
3 _____ _____	3 _____ _____	3 _____ _____
4 _____ _____	4 _____ _____	4 _____ _____

Want

In the second stage of KWL, ask yourself, "What do I **want** to learn as I read?" By doing this you are reading with a purpose (see Review Unit 1).

A Ask yourself what you want to learn as you read "America's Biggest Lottery Winner." Write down some things you hope to learn in the Want column above.

B Before going on to the L in KWL, read the passage "America's Biggest Lottery Winner" on the next page.

America's Biggest Lottery Winner

Jack Whittaker was 57 when he decided to buy a lottery ticket at a small store in West Virginia. A successful businessman who really didn't need to strike it rich, Whittaker
5 played the lottery that day in December of 2002 because the prize was truly a fortune—$314 million. The next morning he learned he had won it all—the largest lottery win in the history of the United States.

10 Whittaker soon surprised everyone with his generosity. He bought property and a car for a worker at the store where he bought the winning ticket. He shared 10 percent of his windfall with his church. He promised to set up a charitable organization to care for the
15 poor of West Virginia. He seemed sensible, saying he'd continue to work at his company and "answer his own phone."

Unfortunately, Whittaker was soon to experience the unforeseen difficulties that come to lottery winners. People would wait for him to drop by his favorite store, and then they would beg him for money—with sad stories of sickness and hard luck. Whittaker had to
20 hire three people just to open letters asking him for money.

Reportedly, he grew extravagant with his money. At a local club, he was seen taking out $50,000—just to impress people. Trips to casinos for gambling grew common. He even shut down his charitable organization. Witnesses said he became a troublemaker at clubs, causing problems and growing irate when refused a request.

25 Whittaker loved his granddaughter, Brandy, immensely—she was "his world," as he said. After winning, Whittaker fulfilled his granddaughter's dreams: a new car and to meet the hip-hop star Nelly. According to Brandy's friend, she had a constant supply of money; it wasn't unusual for her to receive $5,000 in one day from her grandfather. With such money, her lifestyle gradually changed for the worse as she started to use illegal drugs
30 with her friends. Her car was full of trash and money—and bills would occasionally fly out the window, according to another friend.

On December 4, 2003, Brandy disappeared. When they didn't hear from her over the next five days, the Whittakers called the police. Soon after, Brandy's body was found. She had died from taking a large amount of illegal drugs. Whittaker is struggling with health
35 problems. Reports say none of his fortune remains. And the money may have cost him his beloved granddaughter.

Learn

Now that you have finished reading, ask yourself, "What did I **learn** while reading?" Did you learn what you wanted to? This step is similar to the Review and Recite stages of SQ3R (page 139).

A Write down three or four things you learned from "America's Biggest Lottery Winner" in the Learn column of the chart on page 93.

B Now test how much you learned from the passage by answering these questions.

1 Why did Jack Whittaker buy a lottery ticket?
   a. He played the lottery every day.
   b. He knew that he was going to win.
   c. He needed to win money because his business was failing.
   d. The prize was very big.

2 At first, how did Whittaker react to winning $314 million?
   a. He kept all the money for himself.
   b. He quit his job right away.
   c. He was generous with the money.
   d. He gave nearly all of the money away.

3 According to the passage, who told Whittaker stories of sickness and hard luck?
   a. his family
   b. lottery advisers
   c. people begging for money
   d. his granddaughter

4 Why did Whittaker take out $50,000 at a local club?
   a. to impress people
   b. to buy the club
   c. to give it to a friend
   d. to count it

5 Into which paragraph could the following sentence be inserted?: *Sometimes she and her friends would drive around all night long.*
   a. paragraph 2
   b. paragraph 3
   c. paragraph 4
   d. paragraph 5

6 What has happened to Whittaker's fortune?
   a. He still has a lot of it left.
   b. He gave it all to his granddaughter.
   c. None of it remains.
   d. It has grown.

7 What lesson can be inferred from the story of Jack Whittaker?
   a. With enough money, anyone's life is easy.
   b. Time is money.
   c. Money can't buy happiness.
   d. Charity begins at home.

Self Check

Write a short answer to each of the following questions.

1. Have you ever used the KWL method before?

   Yes   No   *I'm not sure.*

2. Do you think KWL is helpful? Why or why not?

3. Will you use KWL on Review Readings 3 and 4? Why or why not?

4. Which of the six reading passages in units 4–6 did you enjoy most? Why?

5. Which of the six reading passages in units 4–6 was easiest? Which was most difficult? Why?

6. When you are reading, do you find yourself having to translate? If yes, what do you think you can do to minimize the translation?

7. What improvements are you making as a reader? Write down one or two things that you know you can do better today than when you started this course.

8. What other improvements do you still want to make as a reader?

Review Reading 3: *Married in a Kimono, Happy in Switzerland*

Fluency Practice

Time yourself as you read through the passage. Try to read as fluently as you can. Record your time in the Reading Rate Chart on page 208. Then answer the questions on the following page.

http://www.ASRculturetalk.com/intercultural

Married in a Kimono, Happy in Switzerland

We interviewed Mayumi, a 36-year-old Japanese woman who has lived in the Swiss town of Bevaix for two years with her husband—an Englishman whom she met on the banks of Lake Neuchâtel

5 in Switzerland.

"In Japan, to answer someone with a 'no' is very impolite. We almost never say it!" said Mayumi. She is thinking back to how she kept this custom even upon her arrival in Switzerland. "The Japanese manage not to ask direct questions

10 in order not to embarrass the person they are speaking with. But here, people ask very directly, 'Do you want a glass of wine?' 'Would you like some coffee?' Well, I always felt I had to say 'yes'!"

Mayumi first set herself up in the city of Montreux, that spectacular resort town on the banks of Lake Geneva. She wanted to finish her education as a tour guide, and she thought

15 that she would be able to communicate with Swiss people in English. "But here, relatively few people speak English!" she told us. However, she was able to find someone who indeed spoke English very well—her future husband, who was an Englishman.

The couple has been married for two years. They live in an extremely modern house in Bevaix, where Mayumi spends most of her time. She has become a mother, and she

20 interrupted her studies to have her second child, a little girl whose name translates as

"purity." Naming a child isn't taken lightly in Japan, and Mayumi had her mother consult a specialist to make sure her choice of name was a good one. Mayumi's roots are in the city of Izumo, west of

25 Osaka. Her brother and her parents still live in the same place, under the same roof. In Japan, tradition says that the eldest son and his wife should come to live in his parents' house with his parents.

30 Mayumi certainly could have been married back in Japan. She refused three proposals of marriage there. Her mother, on the other hand, was married before she was 20. According to the institution of arranged marriages, she knew from when she was a little girl that her parents, Mayumi's grandparents, would choose a husband for her.

Mayumi is both modern and traditional. She raises her children to have Japanese manners.
35 Her son, at 20 months of age, modestly bows his head with his hands folded before every meal. Mayumi told us, "It is a way of showing respect for the family that provided the food. The elder members of the family sit at the top of the Japanese family. In Japan, people who work hard to support the family are shown respect." Mayumi can remember her brother coming home from work each night at 10:00 P.M. "We have very few vacation
40 days, and it's very rare to have a week off," says Mayumi. When her brother attended her wedding in Switzerland, he had to leave the very next day. On her wedding day, she dressed up in a kimono of beautiful Japanese fabric.

Mayumi doesn't think about going back to live in Japan. "I prefer to raise my children here. In Japan, education is so competitive and severe. Furthermore, my husband would
45 never want to live there—there would be too many new rules to learn!" However, Mayumi holds things associated with Japan close to her heart. During her teen years, she studied calligraphy (the art of writing), the tea ceremony, as well as the Japanese version of flower arranging. She is also an expert cook, and she shows off her Japanese dishes to her Swiss friends who are eager to learn from her.

609 words   Time taken _____

Reading Comprehension

1 Why is this passage titled "Married in a Kimono, Happy in Switzerland"?
   a. Clothing is important in both Japan and Switzerland.
   b. Mayumi respects Japanese traditions, but she likes living in Switzerland.
   c. Swiss and Japanese traditions are growing closer.
   d. Mayumi was a very stylish bride at her Swiss wedding.

2 Why did Mayumi always say "yes"?
   a. She learned in Japan that it was impolite to say "no."
   b. She enjoys coffee and wine very much.
   c. She wanted to follow the customs of Switzerland.
   d. Because in Japan, "yes" means "no."

3 Why does Mayumi's brother still live with her parents?
   a. He was never able to find a job he liked.
   b. His wife's parents didn't have room in their house.
   c. It's traditional in Japan for the eldest son to live at home.
   d. His parents didn't want him to move to Switzerland.

4 Which statement is true about Mayumi's mother?
   a. She refused three marriage proposals.
   b. Her parents chose her husband for her.
   c. Her mother was married after the age of 20.
   d. She was married in Switzerland.

5 According to the passage, why does Mayumi's son bow his head before meals?
   a. He is giving thanks to God.
   b. He is showing respect for the food.
   c. He is remembering the hungry children of the world.
   d. He is showing respect for his family.

6 What can we infer from the fact that Mayumi's brother left the day after her wedding?
   a. He doesn't like Switzerland very much.
   b. He had a fight with Mayumi's new husband.
   c. He couldn't change his flight.
   d. He couldn't take any more time off work.

7 Which statement best describes Mayumi's attitude to her home country of Japan?
   a. She loves everything about it and is sorry she can't go back.
   b. She is very glad she left it and doesn't want to go back.
   c. She likes many things about it but doesn't want to go back.
   d. She likes some things about it and wants to go back.

Review Reading 4: The Truth Behind *The Da Vinci Code*

Time yourself as you read through the passage. Try to read as fluently as you can. Record your time in the Reading Rate Chart on page 208. Then answer the questions on the following page.

In 2006, Sony Pictures released a remarkable and intriguing film entitled *The Da Vinci Code*, based on the novel of the same name by Dan Brown. In the film, religious leaders and professors are in a race to discover the secrets of an organization called the Priory of Sion. The biggest secret kept by this organization is supposedly that

5   Jesus Christ and a woman whose name is recorded in the Bible as Mary Magdalene had a child, and that their family line continues to this day. In a TV interview, Dan Brown stated that, in his book, "all of the art, architecture, secret rituals, secret societies, all of that is historical fact." However, while the Priory of Sion did exist, it's nothing like the one which is so central to *The Da Vinci Code*.

10 The Priory of Sion was started in France in 1956 by a skillful liar named Pierre Plantard. *Priory* means religious house, and *Sion* was a hill in the town of Annemasse, where the Priory was started by Plantard and four of his friends. At first, their group fought for housing rights for local people, and their offices were at Plantard's apartment. The organization promised to benefit the weak and the oppressed, and to

15 do good in general. However, there was a darker side to Plantard's Priory.

Plantard actually hoped to use the Priory of Sion to claim to be a descendant of French kings. Between the years 1961 and 1984, Plantard created the enigma of a much more powerful Priory than his insignificant organization. First, in order to give the impression that the Priory began in 1099, Plantard and his friend Philippe de

20 Cherisey created documents, called the *Secret Dossiers of Henri Lobineau*, and

illegally put them into the National Library of France. Next, Plantard got author Gérard de Sède to write a book in 1967 using the false documents; the book became very popular in France. This phenomenon is similar to the popularity of *The Da Vinci Code*, where a book based on false information or speculation becomes popular.

25 Matters were complicated when in 1969, an English actor and science-fiction writer named Henry Lincoln read Gérard de Sède's book. Lincoln did not know of Plantard and his schemes, and may have been a victim of the hoax. He seemed to believe what he read, and jumped to even more wild conclusions, which he published in his 1982 book, *The Holy Blood and the Holy Grail*. He and his co-authors declared as
30 fact that the Priory started in 1099; that its leaders included Leonardo Da Vinci, Isaac Newton, and Victor Hugo; that the Priory protects the descendants of Jesus Christ and Mary Magdalene; and that these descendants ruled France from A.D. 447 to 751. All this was based on reading a novel based on the false facts from documents which were a hoax. Most modern historians do not consider Lincoln's book to be a serious
35 work of history.

How can we be so sure that Plantard created this hoax? Well, the best witness to a crime is the criminal himself. Over 100 hundred letters between Plantard, de Cherisey, and de Sède, discovered by researcher Jean-Luc Chaumeil, show clearly that they were trying to pull an elaborate hoax. In fact, in the 1990s, Plantard got in
40 trouble with the law, and his house was searched. Within it were found many false documents, most harmless, some of which said he was the true king of France. As a final embarrassment, Plantard had to swear in a court of law that the enigma of the Priory of Sion was the work of his imagination.

613 words   Time taken _____

Reading Comprehension

1 What does the author hope to show in this passage?
   a. The Priory of Sion was a hoax.
   b. *The Da Vinci Code* is based on fact.
   c. Dan Brown knew his book wasn't based on fact.
   d. Sony's movie *The Da Vinci Code* is better than Dan Brown's book.

2 What is true about the real Priory of Sion?
   a. It has a secret about Jesus Christ and Mary Magdalene.
   b. Its leader used to be Leonardo Da Vinci.
   c. It was started in 1956 by Pierre Plantard.
   d. It is connected to the leaders of France.

3 Why did Plantard put documents in the National Library of France?
   a. He wanted people to believe that the Priory began in 1099.
   b. He wanted Henry Lincoln to find them there.
   c. So that Gérard de Sède's book would sell more copies.
   d. He believed that he knew the truth and wanted to tell everyone.

4 According to the passage, who did NOT know about the creation of the Priory of Sion hoax?
   a. Gérard de Sède
   b. Philippe de Cherisey
   c. Henry Lincoln
   d. Pierre Plantard

5 Which claim was NOT made in *The Holy Blood and the Holy Grail*?
   a. The Priory of Sion began in 1099.
   b. Isaac Newton was a leader of the Priory of Sion.
   c. Pierre Plantard created the *Secret Dossiers of Henri Lobineau*.
   d. The Priory of Sion protects the descendants of Jesus Christ.

6 Into which paragraph could the following sentence best be inserted?: *Chaumeil had been a member of the Priory until he left it in 1970.*
   a. paragraph 2
   b. paragraph 3
   c. paragraph 4
   d. paragraph 5

7 Why is the author very sure that Plantard is a liar?
   a. *The Da Vinci Code* is too difficult to believe.
   b. Plantard himself said that the Priory was a hoax.
   c. Plantard doesn't seem like a king.
   d. Plantard's claims cannot be found in the Bible.

Getting Ready

Complete the survey below. Compare your answers with a partner.

HEALTHY HABITS QUIZ

Do you . . .	Yes	No	Sometimes
have regularly scheduled mealtimes at home?			
eat meals with family or friends at least once a day?			
plan snacks?			
tailor portion sizes to your needs?			
eat three meals every day?			
try to make mealtimes enjoyable?			
not feel forced to eat everything on your plate?			
make meals last more than 15 minutes?			
eat only in designated areas of the house?			
avoid using food to reward yourself?			
enjoy physical activities once or twice a week?			

Yes = 2 points   **Sometimes** = 1 point   **No** = 0 points

If your total score is:

20–22: You are on the right track. Continue your healthy eating and physical activity habits.

13–19: You are doing well, but you could work on areas where you answered no/sometimes.

12 or lower: Follow the advice above to try to develop healthy habits.

Source: The American Diabetic Association

Unit 7 — Chapter 1: Successful Dieting

Before You Read:
Fad Diets

A Look at these dieting ideas. How effective do you think each one would be for losing weight? Rank them from 1 (most effective) to 5 (least effective).

1 _____ **The Meat Diet:** By eating mainly meat and avoiding carbohydrates you will eventually lose weight.

2 _____ **The Chicken Soup Diet:** You eat breakfast every day, and then you eat as much chicken soup as you want during the rest of the day.

3 _____ **The Cabbage Soup Diet:** Some days vegetables are allowed, on other days beef is allowed, but whenever you are hungry have all the cabbage soup you want.

4 _____ **The Slow Chew Diet:** Chew each mouthful of food 50 times before you swallow it. This will help you enjoy food more and you will need to eat less of it.

5 _____ **The One Meal Diet:** You can have only one meal a day. You can eat whatever you want for that meal and as much as you want.

B Compare and discuss your answers with a partner.

C What other dieting ideas do you know? Share them with a partner.

Reading Skill:
Scanning

When we need to find certain information in a text, we move our eyes quickly across the page. When we see the part of the text that might have our information, we read only that section. This allows us to save time on tests, when searching for information on the Internet, etc.

A Which person gave JudyGirl these pieces of advice? Scan the reading passage to find each piece of advice. Then match the advice with a name.

Advice
1 no white foods _____
2 portion control _____
3 a vegetarian diet _____
4 exercise _____

Person
a. JimGym
b. Minjoo
c. DrewT
d. QueenMother

B Compare your answers with a partner.

C Read the passage again, then answer the questions that follow.

http://www.asrdietforum.com

ASR Diet Forum

Hi,

A question for you **veteran** dieters out there: What's the best way to lose weight and keep it off? I've tried all kinds of **fad** diets: low fat, low
5 **carbohydrate**, grapefruit, cabbage soup, you name it. I've always lost some weight, but I've never been able to keep it off. How do you do it?
JudyGirl, Spokane, Washington

Hi JudyGirl,

10 Fad diets haven't **done the trick** for me, either. The problem is that either you eat too much of one kind of food and get **fed up with** it, or you don't get enough of the foods that your body needs. So when you stop, you eat too much of the foods that weren't on the diet and the weight comes back. For me the solution has been **portion** control. I eat less but enjoy it more. For example, for dinner, I'll fix a nice, attractive meal and put everything in front of me. I'll have a piece of meat, a cooked
15 vegetable, and a salad. Everything is in **moderate** amounts but it looks great. I sit down and eat the meal slowly, and I stop when it's finished. No seconds! And no eating between meals! This method has really worked for me.
DrewT, Chicago

JudyGirl,

20 My secret to weight control has been "no white foods." You know, no white bread, pasta, potatoes, or desserts made with white flour and refined sugar. These foods have a lot of calories but don't contain much nutrition. You can still eat foods made with whole grains like whole wheat bread, crackers, and oatmeal. These foods are better for you, and they fill you up because they contain a lot of **fiber**. So think brown foods, not white!
25 QueenMother, London

Hi JudyGirl,

In your message you didn't say anything about exercise. As I'm sure you're aware, food is only part of the problem for overweight people. Many of us just don't exercise enough.
That was my problem, anyway. I always had a pretty good diet, but I never exercised. Then I went to
30 a weight-loss clinic, and they asked us about our diet and exercise patterns. A counselor there said I should start exercising regularly, both for my weight and general health.
So I joined a gym and started to lift weights several times a week. Now I **alternate** lifting weights, swimming, and jogging. Exercise has made a huge difference in my life. I was able to lose 30 pounds, and I haven't changed my diet very much (though I eat fewer desserts). Also, I've kept off the weight
35 for three years now.
JimGym, Sydney

JudyGirl,

Have you thought about becoming a vegetarian?

I used to eat a lot of meat. Actually, I just ate a normal American diet, but I ate too much junk food. I
40 loved fast-food hamburgers! I wasn't terribly overweight—maybe 25 to 30 pounds,[1] but I still felt too
heavy. Then a friend told me about the health benefits of a vegetarian diet, and I decided to try it. I
didn't lose a lot of weight right away, but I kept losing slowly, maybe a couple of pounds a month.
Now I'm down to my ideal weight (about 145 pounds).

I have to say that it isn't always easy to be a vegetarian. Sometimes it's hard to get a good meal in
45 restaurants, and you have to plan your meals more carefully. But, it's been worth it for me. I look
better, and I feel great!

Minjoo, San Francisco

Hi everybody,

Many thanks to all of you for your great ideas. DrewT and QueenMother, I'm definitely going to try
50 portion control and cut down on white foods. And a special appreciation to you, JimGym. You've
reminded me that I really need to exercise more.

Well, everyone, thanks to you I'm ready to try again. Wish me luck!

Love,

JudyGirl

---

25 to 30 pounds 1 pound = 0.45 kilograms

Reading Comprehension:
Check Your Understanding

A Complete the sentences with information from the reading. Write no more than three words for each answer.

1 JudyGirl is writing in order to get advice on dieting because, although she has been able to lose some weight, she hasn't been able to _____.
2 Thanks to portion control, DrewT eats less food but _____.
3 Although QueenMother doesn't eat white bread, she does eat _____ bread.
4 JimGym points out that food is _____ of the problem.
5 Minjoo thinks that sometimes it's difficult to get _____ in restaurants.

B Choose the best answer to complete each question or statement below.

1 DrewT doesn't eat _____.
   a. meat   b. slowly   c. between meals
2 Which is not an example of a "white food"?
   a. refined sugar   b. oatmeal   c. white bread
3 What did a counselor at a weight-loss clinic recommend to JimGym?
   a. start exercising   b. eliminate desserts   c. stop smoking
4 What kind of fast food did Minjoo used to love?
   a. French fries   b. hamburgers   c. chicken sandwiches
5 Whose advice did JudyGirl not decide to follow?
   a. QueenMother's   b. JimGym's   c. Minjoo's

C Critical Thinking

Discuss these questions with a partner.

1 Would you post a question on the Internet in order to get advice? Why or why not?
2 Which advice that JudyGirl received do you think is the most useful?
3 Have you ever considered becoming a vegetarian? Why or why not?

A Look at the list of words and phrases from the reading. Match each with a definition on the right.

1 alternate _____
2 carbohydrate _____
3 do the trick _____
4 fad _____
5 fed up with _____
6 fiber _____
7 moderate _____
8 portion _____
9 veteran _____

a. sugar or starch found in foods
b. to be effective
c. an experienced person
d. the amount of a food served
e. to change from one thing to another
f. tired of; disgusted with
g. medium or average in amount
h. a fashion or trend, usually short lived
i. part of plants that is healthy to eat, yet cannot actually be digested

B Complete the sentences below using the vocabulary from A. Be sure to use the correct form of the word.

1 The key to a healthy diet is to eat a _____ amount of food each day: not too much and not too little.
2 In order to avoid injury, computer users should _____ between using their right hand and their left hand to operate the mouse.
3 Aspirin didn't help my headache, but that massage you gave me _____. I feel great now.
4 Be sensible about the size of the _____ of food you eat. Serve yourself only what you need, not more.
5 Cookies and candy have lots of _____ that give you quick energy.
6 The hula hoop was a _____ in the 1950s and '60s. It was very popular for a time, but then it disappeared.
7 The old politician was a _____ in the parliament. He had been there for 26 years.
8 I'm _____ the rising cost of living and the high prices of property in this city! I've decided to move to the country!
9 I know you don't like vegetables, Ken, but the doctor said you need to get more _____ in your diet.

Vocabulary Skill:
Creating Word Webs

One helpful strategy that you can use to memorize new vocabulary is to create a "word web." Word webs can help you remember the meaning of new vocabulary and relate this vocabulary to other words you know.

A Complete the diagram below using the words in the box. Then, add other words or phrases you know.

walk more   fatty foods   lots of carbohydrates
fiber   join a gym   moderate portions

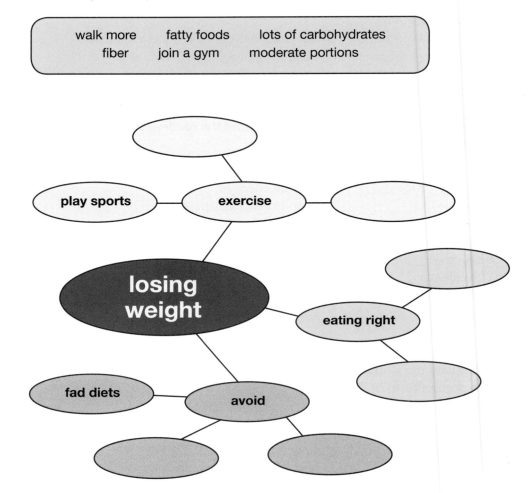

B Explain your diagram to a partner. Add additional words or phrases to your word web.

Chapter 2: Survival at the South Pole

A How much do you know about Antarctica? Choose the best answer for each question or statement below.

1 Of the seven continents on earth, Antarctica is the _____ largest.
   a. third   **b.** fourth   **c.** fifth
2 In what year was Antarctica discovered?
   a. 1720   **b.** 1820   **c.** 1920
3 The first person to reach the South Pole was from _____.
   a. Norway   **b.** Russia   **c.** Argentina
4 Which species of animal is not found in Antarctica?
   a. penguins   **b.** seals   **c.** caribou
5 About how thick is the ice at the South Pole?
   a. 500 meters   **b.** 1,500 meters   **c.** 3,000 meters
6 The coldest outdoor temperature ever measured on Earth was _____, measured in Antarctica.
   a. –50°C   **b.** –70°C   **c.** –90°C

B Compare your answers with a partner.

A How much can you predict about the reading passage? Choose the answer you think is correct.

1 Where do events in the story mainly take place?
   a. on an Antarctic base   **b.** on a fishing boat
2 The woman who appears in the photograph is a _____.
   a. doctor   **b.** explorer
3 The woman battles for survival in a fight with _____.
   a. the cold   **b.** cancer
4 Supplies were sent to the woman by _____.
   a. dogsled   **b.** airplane
5 What did the woman do after returning home?
   a. wrote a book   **b.** retired

B Now skim the reading passage to see whether your predictions in A were correct.

C Read through the passage, then answer the questions that follow.

When good readers approach a text, they start asking themselves questions about it right away, even before they start to read. Predicting activates our previous knowledge of the topic and helps us read more effectively.

Survival at the South Pole

by Mary Ann Vasquez,
DAILY TRIBUNE

In the blackness of the freezing July sky over the South Pole, boxes of medical equipment and food were dropped from a cargo jet. The crates fell through the minus 60 degree air down to an
5 area on the snowy surface lit by burning barrels of fuel. People ran out to collect the boxes. One had smashed on impact, and they **frantically** gathered up the fresh fruit and vegetables before everything froze solid.

10 The staff of 41 people who kept the Amundsen-Scott South Pole Station open that year were extremely **grateful** for the supplies. The station, which sits on 3,000 meters of ice, is in darkness from March to September. The staff usually
15 remains without contact from the outside world during this period of darkness. In the conditions of extreme cold and high winds, even aircraft fuel can freeze, and making a landing to bring people out would be **reckless**. Even air drops of supplies
20 like this one are **undertaken** only in emergency situations. Just such an emergency situation had arisen.

Working under conditions like these is extremely demanding both physically and mentally. When
25 a year before, Jerri Nielsen, M.D.,[1] had seen an advertisement in a medical journal looking for doctors to work at the Amundsen-Scott South Pole Station, she was intrigued. She applied for the position and talked things over with her
30 family. When the position was offered to her, she made the decision to accept it. By November of 1998, Nielsen was settling into her new home for the year—an orange metal shack in Antarctica, which also doubled as her clinic.

35 It was in March of the next year, just a few weeks after the onset of the season of darkness, that Nielsen discovered a mysterious lump in one of her breasts. She had had such lumps before, and hoped that this one, too, would prove to be **innocuous**.
40 Unfortunately, the lump began to grow noticeably, and it was clear that it would need medical attention. Nielsen was the only doctor at the Antarctic base, and she found herself in the strange situation of having to be her own patient.

45 She kept the **tumor** secret from her colleagues, but during the following months the lump grew to the size of a chicken egg. In June, she decided to inform her **supervisor**. Two days later, after exchanging e-mails with the Denver-based doctor
50 in charge of the Antarctic medical programs, a colleague helped Nielsen perform **initial** tests. Using only ice to numb the area, a needle was inserted into the lump in an attempt to **draw out** fluid. When no fluid came out, Nielsen knew the
55 lump was cancerous.

Over the next few months, Nielsen relied on e-mails from doctors in the United States for medical support, and from her family for emotional support. Necessary medical supplies and cancer-fighting drugs were successfully airdropped and Nielsen, with the help of her colleagues and doctors over the Internet, began treatment to fight the disease. At first, the tumor shrank dramatically. Soon, however, it began to enlarge again.

On October 16, 1999, seven months after discovering the lump, Nielsen and another ailing colleague were picked up from the South Pole in the coldest landing ever attempted there, and a replacement physician was dropped off.

Nielsen had the lump removed back in the United States. Medical tests showed that the cancer had not spread to other parts of her body. Thanks to her remarkable colleagues and the Internet, Nielsen made it home alive and, in 2001, published a book about her amazing experience.

¹**M.D.** doctor of medicine

Decide whether the following statements about the reading are true (T) or false (F). If you check (✔) false, correct the statement to make it true.

Reading Comprehension:
Check Your Understanding

	T	F
1 Jerri Nielsen is an American doctor who lived in Antarctica for almost a year.		
2 Antarctica is in darkness from March to December.		
3 Nielsen had never had a lump in her breast before.		
4 Doctors were able to help Nielsen by e-mail.		
5 At first, after treatment started, Nielsen's tumor shrank.		

B **Complete each sentence about the reading with the correct answer, then discuss your answers with a partner.**

1 The staff of the Amundsen-Scott South Pole Station must live without contact from _____.

2 In the extreme cold environment of Antarctica, even airplane fuel can _____.

3 By the time she told her supervisor about it, Nielsen's tumor had grown to the size of a _____.

4 Nielsen was finally able to leave the Antarctic base on _____, 1999.

C Critical Thinking

Discuss these questions with a partner.

1 Why do you think Jerri Nielsen wanted to go to the South Pole in the first place?

2 Why do the United States and many other countries maintain bases in Antarctica?

3 Would you like to live for a time in Antarctica? Why or why not?

Vocabulary Comprehension:
Odd Word Out

A For each group, circle the word that does not belong. The words in *italics* are vocabulary items from the reading.

1 *draw out*	extract	remove	put out
2 anxiously	*frantically*	crazily	intentionally
3 thankful	affluent	*grateful*	appreciative
4 isolated	first	original	*initial*
5 *innocuous*	unforeseen	harmless	safe
6 veteran	*supervisor*	boss	manager
7 wild	mild	*reckless*	uncontrolled
8 cancer	growth	fiber	*tumor*
9 *undertake*	carry out	take on	shirk

B Complete the sentences using the words in *italics* from A. Be sure to use the correct form of the word.

1 It's important to say "thank you" to show that you are _____ for something.

2 Fred is a terribly _____ driver, so I never get in the car with him.

3 After the examination, doctors told Pat that they had discovered a cancerous _____.

4 When my daughter asked my permission to go abroad, my _____ answer was no, but later I changed my mind.

5 The doctor _____ some blood from my arm for testing.

6 The project was too big for any private company; only the government had the resources to _____ it.

7 One of my coworkers was promoted to _____ this week.

8 While some snakes are dangerous, the ones in my garden are completely _____.

9 David searched _____ for his passport as his flight was getting ready to leave.

A What do you think the following words mean? Use each word to complete the sentences below.

> overcook   overcome   overdue   overtime
> understaffed   underground   underwear

1 We need to pay these bills today. They are two weeks _____.
2 Beneath the city of London, there are many _____ passages that were used during World War II.
3 Four teachers have left the university, so now the English department is _____.
4 The restaurant was very busy this week, so Fumiko had to work ten hours _____.
5 Don't _____ the chicken or it will be too dry to eat.
6 If you want to stay really warm during the winter, I suggest wearing wool clothes and silk _____.
7 One way to _____ the desire to smoke is to chew gum.

B Now use either *over-* or *under-* to complete the sentences below. Check your answers with a partner.

1 If you let stress _____power you, you'll get so nervous you won't be able to do anything.
2 Jorge is 183 centimeters tall, but he's several kilos _____weight. He weighs only 70 kg.
3 Poor Yuko is terribly _____worked. She should work only from 9:00 to 5:00, but most days she works until 8:00 or 9:00.
4 Simon poured the tea into the cup too quickly, and it _____flowed onto the table.
5 Carla is _____paid. She makes $4 per hour, but she really should make more money.
6 What is the capital of Italy? Please _____line the correct answer: Rome, Milan, Venice.

Vocabulary Skill:
The Prefixes *over-* and *under-*

In this chapter you learned the verb "undertake." This word is formed by adding the prefix "under-" to the verb "take." The prefix "over-" can mean "too much" or "more"; the prefix "under-" can mean "too little" or "beneath."

Real Life Skill:
Recognizing Common Medical Abbreviations

In this unit, you read the abbreviation "M.D.," meaning "doctor of medicine." There are many common medical abbreviations used to refer to doctors, places in a hospital, tools used by health specialists, and one's health. These abbreviations are written as well as said; in most cases, when spoken, each letter of the abbreviation is pronounced.

A Practice saying the abbreviations. Then match each abbreviation to its correct meaning.

1 OR •   • a. intensive care unit
2 M.D. •   • b. operating room
3 IV •   • c. deoxyribonucleic acid
4 CPR •   • d. blood pressure
5 HIV •   • e. emergency room
6 OB-GYN •   • f. doctor of medicine
7 ER •   • g. human immunodeficiency virus
8 ICU •   • h. obstetrician-gynecologist
9 DNA •   • i. intravenous injection
10 BP •   • j. cardiopulmonary resuscitation

B Write the appropriate abbreviation from A beside each sentence below. Check your answers with a partner.

1 A person in a car accident will probably be brought here upon reaching the hospital. _____
2 If a person is seriously injured, after surgery he will probably go from the OR to this place in the hospital. _____
3 You'd see this doctor if you were going to have a child. _____
4 You might see this physician once a year for a checkup. _____
5 This causes the disease AIDS. _____
6 If you were unable to drink or eat in a hospital, you might get one of these. _____
7 This is the genetic material that determines what you will look like. _____
8 This shouldn't be higher than 140 over 90. If it is, you may suffer from hypertension. _____
9 A man on the bus collapses and stops breathing. You might do this and save his life. _____

What Do You Think?

1 Do you think people these days worry too much about their weight?
2 What are some of the factors explaining the increasing life expectancy of people?
3 What types of medical treatment do people in your country use to stay healthy or to deal with illness or pain?
4 How would it feel to spend six months in Antarctica? What would you do to pass the time?

Getting Ready

Discuss the following questions with a partner.

1 Name as many of the vehicles pictured above as you can.
2 What important events do you know in the history of flight?
3 Which countries have space programs? What are their accomplishments?
4 Make three predictions about the future of space travel.

Chapter 1: Human Adaptation to Space

Before You Read:
Life in Space

Discuss the following questions with a partner.

1 What do you know about the job of an astronaut? What kind of work does an astronaut do in space?
2 Do you think an astronaut's job is dangerous? Can you remember any accidents involving spaceflight?
3 What do you think are the physical effects of living in space for a long time?
4 Do you think humans should hurry to send people to live in space stations and on other planets?

Reading Skill:
Identifying Main and Supporting Ideas

Most paragraphs have a main idea, or topic, that tells us what that paragraph is about. Often, you will find the main idea talked about in the first or second sentence of a paragraph. Supporting ideas usually follow the main idea. Sentences containing supporting ideas explain or give us more information about the main idea.

A Read the statements below. Write M next to the statement that is the main idea of the paragraph. Write S next to the statement that is a supporting idea.

Paragraph 2
1 Although most astronauts do not spend more than a few months in space, many experience physiological problems when they return to Earth. _____
2 More than two-thirds of all astronauts suffer from motion sickness while traveling in space. _____

Paragraph 3
3 Bone density can decrease at a rate of one percent to two percent a month, and, as a result, many astronauts are unable to walk properly for a few days upon their return to Earth. _____
4 Throughout the duration of a mission, astronauts' bodies experience some potentially dangerous disorders. _____

Paragraph 4
5 In addition to physiological difficulties, astronauts who travel for extended periods may also suffer from psychological stress. _____
6 In addition, long periods away from family and friends can leave space travelers feeling lonely and depressed. _____

B Compare your answers with a partner. Then scan the paragraphs to find the sentences and to find other supporting ideas.

C Now read through the passage, and answer the questions that follow.

Human Adaptation to Space

"It is important for the human race to spread out into space for the survival of the species," said world-renowned astrophysicist Steven Hawking. He is far from being alone in his vision of humans learning to live in places other than on Earth. Movies such as Stanley Kubrick's *2001: A Space Odyssey* explored the possibility of sustaining human life in outer space, and presented a very realistic **portrayal** of spaceflight. Since astronaut Yuri Gagarin became the first man to travel in space in 1961, scientists have researched what conditions are like beyond Earth's atmosphere, and what effects space travel has on the human body.

Although most astronauts do not spend more than a few months in space, many experience **physiological** problems when they return to Earth. Some of these **ailments** are short-lived; others may be long-lasting. More than two-thirds of all astronauts suffer from motion sickness while traveling in space. In the gravity-free environment, the body cannot **distinguish** up from down. The body's internal balance system sends confusing signals to the brain, which can result in nausea[1] lasting as long as a few days. A body that is **deprived** of gravity also experiences changes in the **distribution** of bodily fluids. More fluid than normal ends up in the face, neck, and chest, resulting in a puffy face, bulging neck veins, and a slightly enlarged heart.

Throughout the **duration** of a mission, astronauts' bodies experience some potentially dangerous **disorders**. One of the most common is loss of muscle mass and bone density. Another effect of the weightless environment is that astronauts tend not to use the muscles they rely on in a gravity environment, so the muscles gradually atrophy.[2] This, combined with the shift of fluid to the upper body and the resulting loss of essential minerals such as calcium, causes bones to weaken. Bone density can decrease at a rate of one to two percent a month and, as a result, many astronauts are unable to walk properly for a few days upon their return to Earth. **Exposure** to radiation[3] is another serious hazard that astronauts face. Without the Earth's atmosphere to protect them, astronauts can be exposed to intense radiation from the sun and other galactic bodies,[4] leaving them at risk of cancer.

In addition to physiological difficulties, astronauts who travel for extended periods may also suffer from psychological stress. Astronauts live and work in small, tight spaces, and they must be able to deal with psychological stress caused by the confined environment. In addition, long periods away from family and friends can leave space travelers feeling lonely and depressed.

Now that humans have been to the Moon, and unmanned missions have been sent to Mars, the United States has unveiled plans for a permanent lunar space station and manned missions to and from Mars.

Differences between the orbits[5] of Earth and Mars mean that a round trip between the two planets

35 would take almost three years to complete. The National Space Biomedical Research Institute (NSBRI) is currently investigating the hazards posed by a spaceflight of that duration. While during shorter flights, some of the physical and mental challenges of space travel have been controlled with diet and regular exercise, in the case of long-term space travel it is still not entirely clear how well the human body could adapt or even survive.

40 In 2010, the NSBRI is due to present its findings to NASA[6] and present a "go" or "no go" recommendation regarding manned missions to Mars. As new technologies develop to help scientists further pursue their goals, we may one day see humans walk on distant planets.

[1]**nausea** a feeling of sickness that may cause one to vomit
[2]**atrophy** to become weak; to lose size and strength
[3]**radiation** heat or light from something such as the sun, a microwave, or X-rays that can be harmful to humans
[4]**galactic bodies** other stars and planets in the galaxy
[5]**orbit** the curved path that a planet or space shuttle makes around a star or another planet
[6]**NASA** National Aeronautics and Space Administration, the agency in the United States that is responsible for space exploration and travel

Reading Comprehension:
Check Your Understanding

A Decide whether the following statements about the reading are true (T) or false (F). If you check (✔) false, correct the statement to make it true.

	T	F
1 The topic of this reading passage is how to stay healthy in space.		
2 In 1961 the first astronaut traveled to space.		
3 As a result of weightlessness, astronauts' legs and arms are often swollen with fluid.		
4 A danger astronauts face in space is prolonged contact with cancerous rays from the sun.		
5 The NSBRI has approved a manned mission to Mars.		

B Choose the best answer for each statement below. Try not to look back at the reading for the answers.

1 In *2001: A Space Odyssey*, there is a realistic portrayal of _____.
   a. spaceflight   **b.** planetary motion   **c.** the painful effects of spaceflight
2 Without gravity, the body doesn't know the difference between _____.
   a. right and left   **b.** up and down   **c.** fast and slow
3 Long periods of time in space can leave space travelers feeling _____.
   a. depressed   **b.** energetic   **c.** confused
4 A round trip between Earth and Mars would take about _____.
   a. three years   **b.** five years   **c.** seven years

C Critical Thinking

Discuss these questions with a partner.

1 What do astronauts eat and drink while in space?
2 If a city were created on Mars, would you be willing to go live there?
3 Should the world's nations work together on an international space program?

A

The words in *italics* are vocabulary items from the reading. Read each question or statement and choose the correct answer. Compare your answers with a partner.

Vocabulary Comprehension: Vocabulary in Context

1 If you have a progressive *ailment* you should probably _____.
   a. see a doctor **b.** show it off
2 In which setting might you likely be *deprived* of water?
   a. a beach **b.** a desert
3 A person with an eating *disorder* eats _____ food.
   a. just the right amount of **b.** too little or too much
4 It's often hard to *distinguish* between _____.
   a. mother and daughter **b.** identical twins
5 If there is an even *distribution* of wealth in a country, there is a _____ number of people who are very rich or very poor.
   a. small **b.** large
6 The *duration* of that remarkable phenomenon was _____.
   a. very loud **b.** two hours
7 To protect your skin from *exposure* to the sun, you should wear _____.
   a. a bathing suit **b.** sun screen
8 Which is an example of a *physiological* problem?
   a. poor eyesight **b.** depression
9 I'm fed up with unrealistic *portrayals* of Americans that many people get _____
   a. in 1940s movies **b.** from visiting the United States

B Answer the questions. Share your answers with a partner.

1 What are some *physiological ailments* associated with not eating right?
2 Which actors have done remarkable *portrayals* of historical figures?
3 What are some ways of dealing with a *disorder* causing children not to pay attention at school?
4 What could you do to *distinguish* between two people who look alike?
5 Where else might you be *deprived* of water?
6 Is there an even *distribution* of wealth in your country?
7 How else can you protect your skin from *exposure* to the sun?
8 What is the *duration* of a typical movie?

Vocabulary Skill:

The Prefixes
dis- and *de-*

In this chapter you learned the word "deprived," meaning "without something that is necessary"; you also read the noun "disorder," meaning "an illness" or "something that is not in order." The prefix "de-" means "reduce," "remove," or "not." "Dis-" also means "not," as well as "apart." These are two very common prefixes that come before nouns, verbs, adjectives, and adverbs to form many words in English.

A What do you think the following words mean? Complete the sentences below using the words.

> deduct   detach   discharge
> depart   disgrace

1 At what time is our plane scheduled to _____?
2 The Olympic athlete faced public _____ after it was discovered he'd taken drugs in order to win the competition.
3 When you hand in your application, _____ and return the lower part of the document. Keep the upper part for your records.
4 After serving in the military for two years, Jin Ho received an honorable _____ from the army.
5 If you turn your test paper in late, Professor Yeo will _____ ten points from your score.

B Now use either *de-* or *dis-* to complete the sentences below. Use your dictionary to help you.

1 The plane is about to make its _____scent into Tokyo. We should be arriving in about 20 minutes.
2 When Michiko lit a cigarette in the restaurant and began smoking, the waiter gave her a _____approving look.
3 The smell of fish is awful in here! Is there anything we can do to _____odorize this room?
4 When we get off the plane we have to _____embark through the door on the left.
5 At the end of the concert the crowd began to _____perse, and within 20 minutes almost everyone had left the building.

C Can you think of an antonym for each of the new words you've learned in this exercise? Share your ideas with a partner.

Chapter 2: Pioneers of Flight

A In which order did these things happen in history? Number them in order from 1 to 6.

_____ Airplanes with jet engines are created.

_____ The first gliders are developed.

_____ The first manned rockets are developed.

_____ There is the first manned flight of a hot-air balloon.

_____ The kite is invented.

_____ The first engine-powered aircraft takes flight.

B Discuss the following questions with a partner.

1 What do you think about the following saying: *If people were meant to fly, they would be born with wings.*

2 Have you ever tried hang-gliding? If not, would you like to? Why or why not?

3 What are the names of some people associated with the history of flight?

Reading Skill:
Making Inferences

A Read the passage, then choose the best answer to the questions below. You will have to infer or guess information from the reading.

1 Wan Hu most likely _____.
   a. had a successful flight into space   **b.** was blown up by the explosion

2 One reason the Spruce Goose could have been an improvement over using ships to transport troops is because of _____.
   a. its speed and safety from submarine attack   **b.** its cost and size

3 The Spruce Goose was never used in World War II because _____.
   a. it cost too much to make   **b.** by the time it was finished, the war was over

4 Adrian Nicholas has probably made many _____ before.
   a. parachute jumps   **b.** of Leonardo da Vinci's devices

B Explain your answers in A to a partner.

C Read the passage again, then answer the questions that follow.

Information in a reading passage is not always stated directly. Sometimes a reader has to infer, or make guesses, about events or a writer's opinion or meaning, from the information that is available in the reading.

Pioneers of Flight

The Legend of Wan Hu

China launched its first rocket with human beings aboard on October 15, 2003. Astronaut Yang Liwei brought to its **fulfillment** a dream that probably had its roots in a much earlier time. Although the **veracity** of the story cannot be confirmed, legend has it that in A.D. 1500 a man named Wan Hu prepared his own mission to the
5 stars. At that time, the Chinese invention of gunpowder was widely used in rockets for military purposes as well as in fireworks. Wan Hu devised a risky plan to **harness** the power of such rockets to take him to the stars.

The story goes that Wan Hu built the first spaceship: a chair with 47 powerful gunpowder rockets and two kites attached to it. On the day of the launch, each rocket was lit by a different servant carrying a torch. The servants then moved back and waited. An earth-shattering explosion followed: Wan Hu and his primitive spaceship had
10 disappeared completely. Although the story may seem a little **far-fetched**, the principles of rocket-powered spaceflight are contained in Wan Hu's crazy dream.

Howard Hughes's Spruce Goose

On November 2, 1947, a crowd of onlookers at San Pedro harbor in Los Angeles witnessed aviation history. An
15 enormous flying boat, nicknamed the Spruce Goose, sped across the bay and rose 70 feet above the water. After just under a minute, it landed perfectly one mile down the bay. It was the first and last time the boat ever flew.

The **concept** for construction of the Spruce Goose came
20 from the need for more effective ways of transporting troops and materials in World War II. The idea came from a man called Henry Kaiser, but it was Howard Hughes, the legendary multi-millionaire, who actually developed the flying boat.

The Spruce Goose was the biggest airplane ever built and still holds the record for the greatest wingspan,[1] and it was made entirely of wood. Though it had promise, in the end the project failed for three main reasons:
25 the cost of building the enormous machine; the complexity of working with wood; and Hughes's perfectionist approach, which caused the entire project to finish behind schedule. The Goose was put into storage and remained hidden from view until 1976, when it was put on display for the public. In 1992, the plane was **dismantled** and transported to the state of Oregon, where it remains today. Many of the design features of the Spruce Goose have been incorporated into modern **cargo** planes. Like other **pioneers** in the field of
30 transportation, Hughes was simply ahead of his time.

The Futuristic Ideas of Leonardo da Vinci

Centuries before Hughes was designing the Spruce Goose, another pioneer in transportation design was sketching plans for different kinds of flying machines. Leonardo da Vinci, perhaps the most famous artist of the

Renaissance period, planned flying devices with flapping wings controlled
35 and steered by human pilots. His research focused on the complex anatomy[2] of birds in flight, and he based his flying machines on this **analogy**. It took almost 500 years for da Vinci's sketches to become real. In June 2000, a professional parachutist named Adrian Nicholas jumped out of a hot-air balloon over the South African countryside using a parachute
40 made of wood and canvas based on one of da Vinci's designs. Nicholas landed safely, and Leonardo's dream became reality. These three enigmatic individuals, Wan Hu, Howard Hughes, and Leonardo da Vinci, came from places and cultures that are about as different as we can imagine. What they shared was a fascination with flying, a spirit of innovation, and the
45 courage to try and make their dreams of flight come true.

[1]**wingspan** the distance from the tip of one wing to the tip of the other
[2]**anatomy** structure of the body

A Decide whether the following statements about the reading are true (T) or false (F). If you check (✔) false, correct the statement to make it true.

Reading Comprehension: Check Your Understanding

		T	F
1	The author of the article believes that all three of the individuals are definitely real.		
2	According to the legend, Wan Hu created the first spaceship.		
3	The Spruce Goose made only two flights.		
4	The Spruce Goose is one of the largest airplanes ever built.		
5	Leonardo da Vinci was both an inventor and an artist.		

B Complete the sentences with information from the reading. Write no more than three words for each answer.

1 Wan Hu's spaceship was a chair with two kites and _____.
2 The idea for the Spruce Goose was originally thought of by

  _____.
3 The Spruce Goose was made of _____.
4 Leonardo da Vinci got ideas for flying machines from studying

  _____.
5 Adrian Nicholas jumped out of a _____.

C Critical Thinking

Discuss these questions with a partner.

1 Who else might the author have included in this article? Why?
2 Which of these three pioneers was the most interesting to you?
   Explain your choice.

Vocabulary Comprehension:
Odd Word Out

A For each group, circle the word that does not belong. **The words in *italics* are vocabulary items from the reading.**

1	*fulfillment*	completion	attainment	interpretation
2	correctness	*veracity*	modesty	truth
3	channel	function	*harness*	make use of
4	hard to believe	external	unlikely	*far-fetched*
5	*concept*	union	thought	idea
6	take apart	*dismantle*	ventilate	break down
7	media	baggage	*cargo*	load
8	comparison	similarity	institution	*analogy*
9	*pioneer*	inventor	innovator	supervisor

B Complete the sentences using the words in *italics* from A. Be sure to use the correct form of the word.

1 When the ship hit a rock, its _____ of oil spilled into the sea.
2 When Rick finally struck it rich in the computer business, it was the _____ of a lifelong dream, thanks to 20 years of hard work.
3 I think the idea that human life expectancy will increase to 1,000 years is _____.
4 A common _____ is to compare the human brain to a computer.
5 I find mathematical _____ such as integration difficult to understand.
6 The criminal's story is supposedly true, but I doubt its _____.
7 If we could only _____ the energy of the sun, the world's energy problems would be solved.
8 Medical _____ have developed a cutting-edge method of treating tumors.
9 The stolen car was quickly _____ in the thieves' garage and the parts sold.

A Look at these two idioms related to time. Complete the sentences with the correct idiom. Using the sentences to help you, write a simple definition for *ahead of time.*

ahead of one's time: too modern or forward thinking for the time period one lives in
ahead of time: _____
a. I thought Marcus was coming at 8:00, but he arrived _____ at 7:30.
b. Amelia Earhart was one of the first female aviators. She was truly _____.

B Now do the same for each of the idiom pairs below. Compare your answers with a partner.

1 at a time: in a certain specific number
   at one time: _____
   a. Okay everyone; please enter the theater two _____.
   b. Ms. Yang lived in Taiwan _____, but she doesn't anymore.
2 in no time: _____
   in time: after a certain amount of time has passed, usually a while
   a. We're almost at the beach; it's only about another mile. We'll be there _____.
   b. Don't worry! You'll learn to write well in Chinese _____, but it'll take a while.
3 all the time: happening continuously, regularly
   of all time: _____
   a. I think that Thomas Edison is one of the greatest inventors _____.
   b. My computer keeps crashing _____, and I can't make any progress with this report.
4 for a time: for a short period of time
   for the time being: _____
   a. You can sit at Hannah's desk _____, but when she comes back you'll have to move.
   b. Junko and Koji dated _____, but I don't think they are still together.

In this chapter, you read the idiom "ahead of one's time." An idiom is a fixed group of words that has a special meaning. There are many idioms that are formed using the word "time." Sometimes it's possible to know what the idiom means by looking at the individual words, but it can also be helpful to look at the surrounding words in order to understand its meaning.

Real Life Skill:

Dictionary Usage: Identifying Parts of Speech

When you learn new words in English, it is also helpful to learn their parts of speech so that you understand how to use them in sentences. You can use your dictionary to learn a word's part of speech, as well as related word forms (e.g., stress, stressed, stressful).

A Below are some of the parts of speech that appear in dictionaries. Work with a partner to complete the Description column.

Part of Speech	Example	Description
noun (*n*)	Tom has a lot of **stress** in his life.	person, place, or thing
verb (*v*)	Jessica **studies** Spanish.	
adjective (*adj*)	Fumiko had a **stressful** day. She felt **stressed out**.	
adverb (*adv*)	He read the paper **very carefully.**	
phrasal verb (*phr v*)	Hiromi **handed in** her paper	
conjunction (*conj*)	Where are my hat **and** coat?	joins two or more words, sentences, or ideas
preposition (*prep*)	The cup is **on** the table. Your name is **after** mine on the list.	describes time and location; makes a comparison between things

B Read each sentence. For each italicized word, write the correct part of speech. Use your dictionary to help you.

1 I can't *keep up with* my work this week.   phrasal verb
2 Mark has a *spontaneous* sense of humor.   _____
3 There hasn't been a war here for six *decades*.   _____
4 Hotel prices are cheaper *during* the off-season.   _____
5 Maria is searching *frantically* for her lost keys.   _____
6 The couple *adopted* a child with no parents.   _____
7 I resemble my mother, *but* I don't look like my father at all.   _____
8 Meteorologists *are speculating* about where the storm will hit.   _____
9 One drop of water in the desert is *insignificant*.   _____
10 The gasoline *burst into flame* when the cigarette touched it.   _____

What Do You Think?

1 In what ways will transportation on Earth change in the future?
2 Do you believe that humans must go into space? Why or why not?
3 Who was a pioneer, in any field, whom you admire? Why do you admire that person?
4 If you could have a meeting with that pioneer, what three questions would you like to ask him or her?

The Changing Family

Getting Ready

Discuss the following questions with a partner.

1 Match these terms with the photos above.
   a. nuclear family   **b.** childless couple   **c.** extended family   **d.** single-parent family
2 Explain what each of the terms above means.
3 Do extended families often live under one roof in your country, or are families spread out?
   Explain your answer.
4 Are people having more or fewer children these days? Why?

Chapter 1: Is an Only Child a Lonely Child?

Before You Read:
Family Options

A Look at the opinions below. Check (✔) A if you agree or D if you disagree with the opinion.

		A	D
1	It is better for the extended family to live together.		
2	Parents should always have two children at least.		
3	A childless couple can be happy.		
4	It is better to grow up with many brothers and sisters.		
5	An only child can sometimes be happier than a child who grows up with many brothers and sisters.		
6	It is possible for a family to be too big.		
7	The pressures of modern life are making families smaller.		

B Explain your answers in A to a partner.

Reading Skill:
Recognizing Facts

A fact is something that is always true. Opinions are only sometimes true and are signaled by "in my opinion," "believe," "think," "might," "may," "probably," "should," etc. Knowing the difference between facts and opinions is important when researching controversial topics.

A Are these statements facts? Skim the reading, then scan it to find information about each statement, and check (✔) F (fact) or S (sometimes true) for each.

		F	S
1	Only children feel lonely during vacations.		
2	An only child doesn't have any brothers or sisters to associate with.		
3	An only child is less capable of interacting with people his or her own age.		
4	The number of parents choosing to have only one child is increasing in many parts of the world.		
5	Only children receive more quality time and attention from their parents.		
6	What is appropriate for one family may not be appropriate for another.		

B Compare your answers with a partner.

C Read through the passage again, then answer the questions that follow.

Is an Only Child a Lonely Child?

This month in *Family Planner* magazine, child psychologist Dr. Ethan Wood answers a question from Andrea Gonzales, who writes:

Q: Dear Dr. Wood,

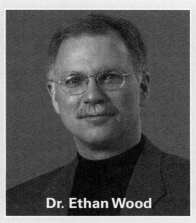

Dr. Ethan Wood

My husband and I are facing a **dilemma**, namely, the issue of whether to have a second child—we already have one healthy, happy five-year-old daughter. Both of us have demanding jobs, and limited time and financial resources, but we're also very keen to make sure that our only child does not become a lonely child. So, what are the pros and cons of having a second child?

A: Dear Andrea,

This is one of the most difficult issues that parents nowadays face.

As you point out, a concern that is often heard with regard to only children is whether one child necessarily means a lonely child. Many parents of only children feel a **stigma** associated with their decision to have only one child. There are no other children in the family for the child to associate with, and this may lead to the child feeling lonely at times, especially during vacations.

Another common argument against having just one child is that an only child may be more spoiled than one with **siblings**. Many people believe that a single child will not have learned to **negotiate** with others, and respect the **give-and-take** involved in many relationships. Some think this may leave the child less capable of interacting well with people his or her own age than one who has been raised with siblings.

Despite these arguments, the number of parents choosing to have only one child is increasing in many parts of the world. In South Korea, the percentage of families with only one child is higher than ever. In fact, the average number of children per couple has fallen to 1.19 children—significantly below the replacement level of 2.1 children. This follows a general trend in Asia where in many countries, e.g., Japan, China, Singapore, Taiwan, and Thailand, couples are having on average fewer than two children. In Japan, the average number of children born per family had declined to 1.25 by 2005. This has led to government concerns about supporting an increasing population of elderly people in the future; it is predicted that by 2020, a third of the population in Japan will be aged 65 or over. For some single-child parents, particularly those with busy careers, the pressures of devoting time and energy to a second child can seem too **overwhelming**, resulting in them **electing** to have no more children. For other parents, the financial burden of having a second child may be the **prime** consideration. Another important consideration is the increasing age at which women are getting married. Pregnancy and childbirth can be exceedingly demanding even on a young mother. Women in their 30s may choose not to go through it a second time, or can even have fertility[1] issues.

Advocates of single-child families argue that there are advantages for the child as well as the parents. With just one child, they suggest, there is less potential for family arguments arising from favoritism or sibling jealousy. Moreover, with only one child, the parents can give, and the child can receive, more quality time and attention. This often leads to increased **self-esteem**, which, combined with increased independence, can lead to the child being more confident. Unfortunately, Andrea, there is no simple answer to the question of whether or not to have a second child. The circumstances affecting each set of parents are unique, and what is appropriate for one family may not be for another. The important thing, in the end, is to make a decision that both you and your husband feel confident about.

40

¹**fertility** the ability to produce children

Reading Comprehension:
Check Your Understanding

A Choose the best answer for each question or statement about the reading below. Try not to look back at the reading for the answers.

1 Andrea wants to make sure that her child isn't _____.
   a. forgotten   **b.** uneducated   **c.** lonely
2 An argument against having only one child is that the child will be _____.
   a. sad   **b.** spoiled   **c.** easily frightened
3 The replacement level for a population is _____ children per couple.
   a. 2.1   **b.** 2   **c.** 1.9
4 Advocates of having only one child suggest that only children don't have to deal with the problem of _____.
   a. bad grades   **b.** loneliness   **c.** favoritism

B Decide whether the following statements about the reading are true (T) or false (F). If you check (✔) false, correct the statement to make it true.

	T	F
1 Andrea Gonzales's husband works; she is a housewife.		
2 Some people believe that only children are spoiled because they don't receive enough attention from adults.		
3 The Japanese government fears that the elderly won't have people to care for them in the future.		
4 Money worries can be a reason for choosing not to have more children.		
5 Dr. Wood suggests that Andrea Gonzales and her husband should probably not have another child.		

C Critical Thinking

Discuss these questions with a partner.

1 If you were Andrea, what would you decide to do?
2 Do you think the population of the world will go down in the future, or will it continue to rise? Why do you think so?

A For each group, circle the word that does not belong. The words in *italics* are vocabulary items from the reading.

1 *dilemma*	solution	problem	difficult choice
2 choose	*elect*	adopt	select
3 cooperation	demand	*give-and-take*	mutual assistance
4 compromise	insist	cooperate	*negotiate*
5 *overwhelm*	draw out	overpower	beat
6 first	*prime*	secondary	main
7 self-confidence	self-worth	*self-esteem*	selfishness
8 brother	sister	veteran	*sibling*
9 *stigma*	shame	pride	disgrace

B Complete the letter below using the words in *italics* from A. Be sure to use the correct form of the word.

Dear Dr. Wood,

I read with interest your reply to Andrea Gonzales about whether or not she and her husband should have another child. I, too, am facing a similar (1)_____ related to having children; my fiancé wants us to start a family after we are married, but I don't. I do realize that marriage is all about (2)_____, but this is one thing I am not willing to (3)_____. I don't want to be a mother. My (4)_____ reason for not wanting to be a parent is because I am a 28-year-old woman who has a demanding job as an artist—which I love. I have (5)_____ to put all of my emotional and financial resources into developing my career rather than having children. To add the responsibilities of children to my already busy life would be (6)_____. Unfortunately, my fiancé does not feel the same way (he comes from a large family and has many (7)_____), nor, to my surprise, do many of my female friends. You can't imagine the (8)_____ attached to being a woman who says she doesn't want children. Honestly, some people look at me like I'm a monster! Though I have strong feelings about this, I must admit my (9)_____ has suffered terribly in the past few months; I sometimes wonder if I am making the right decision. If I choose not to have children, I know, too, that my fiancé will probably not want to get married. What should I do?

Mariah
Miami, Florida

Vocabulary Skill:
Compound Nouns

In this chapter, you learned the compound nouns "give-and-take" and "self-esteem." Compound nouns are two or more nouns, adjectives, adverbs, or verbs that work together to talk about one person, place, or thing.

A Look at how compound nouns are formed. What parts of speech are joined together to form each?

1   Some compound nouns join two words together to form one word.
a low *birthrate*   children's *software*   Let's eat *takeout*.

2   Some compound nouns are two words that work together to refer to one thing.
family planning   maternity leave   family tree

3   Some compound nouns are formed by joining two or more words together with hyphens.
high *self-esteem*   a lot of *give-and-take*   John's *mother-in-law*

B Join one word from the box with a word below to form a compound noun. Is each compound written as one word or two words, or is it hyphenated? Use your dictionary to help you.

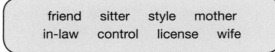

friend   sitter   style   mother
in-law   control   license   wife

1   father _____
2   boy _____
3   self _____
4   baby _____
5   driver's _____
6   house _____
7   grand _____
8   life _____

C Match each compound noun with the correct definition below.

1   a person who takes care of children while the parents are out
_____

2   a woman who stays home and takes care of the house and children
_____

3   one's male companion or lover _____
4   the male parent of one's spouse _____
5   your father's or mother's mother _____
6   one's chosen way of living _____
7   legal permission to use a car _____
8   the ability to remain calm and not show one's feelings; will power
_____

Chapter 2: Changing Roles: Stay-at-Home Dads

A Whom do you usually associate these family responsibilities with? Write W for women, M for men, or B for both.

1 making money _____
2 cleaning the house _____
3 doing the laundry _____
4 paying the bills _____
5 disciplining children _____
6 cooking meals _____
7 caring for children _____
8 fixing things _____
9 driving places _____
10 entertaining guests _____

B Compare your answers with a partner. Explain any answers that differ.

A Take one minute to preview the reading passage. Think about the title and the picture, scan the passage for interesting information, and skim the beginning and ending paragraphs.

B Now discuss these questions about the reading passage with a partner.

1 What do you think the passage is about?
2 Where could you find this kind of an article?
3 What do you already know about this subject?
4 What interesting points did you notice?
5 Do you think you'll enjoy reading the passage?

C Now read through the passage, then answer the questions that follow.

Before You Read:
Family Responsibilities

Reading Skill:
Previewing

Previewing is something good readers do when they first encounter new reading material. They ask themselves questions like these: *What is this about? What kind of text is this? What do I already know about it?* Previewing can involve skimming, scanning, and predicting to help us get acquainted with the reading passage.

Changing Roles: Stay-at-Home Dads

As little as 30 years ago, few people questioned the gender roles that had prevailed for centuries. The conventional wisdom[1] was that a woman's place was in the home, and that a man's main responsibility to his family was to put
5 food on the table. In the 1970s and '80s, however, greater numbers of working women meant that men were no longer the sole[2] **breadwinners**. A father's involvement with his family also became more important. Forty years ago, almost no husbands were "stay-at-home dads." Today, with more career opportunities than
10 ever available to women, the stay-at-home dad trend is on the rise.

A family with a stay-at-home dad can **reap** many benefits. If the wife is a career-woman, her husband can take some family responsibilities off her shoulders, thereby allowing her to compete more successfully with career-minded men. Being the main caregiver to the children allows men the joy of participating in their children's day-to-day experiences. Studies have also found that
15 the presence of the father in the home can contribute to lower **juvenile** crime rates, a decrease in child poverty, and lower rates of teenage pregnancy. Differences in parenting styles between men and women are also believed to contribute to children's ability to understand and communicate emotions in different ways. The research supports claims by some groups that the absence of a father in the family is the single biggest social problem in modern society.

20 ## Case 1: Masato Yamada
Nonetheless, many men have found opposition from the corporate world to their decision to become stay-at-home dads. Masato Yamada and his wife, Atsuko, worked at Japan's busy trade ministry. Atsuko had twins, and took maternity leave[3] to take care of them. When Atsuko later had a third child, Masato decided to request paternity leave[4] to be the children's primary
25 caregiver. His boss's initial reaction was, "Are you serious?" While he was, in the end, given permission, he was lucky. A recent Japanese government survey showed that only 6.5 percent of fathers who have young children were able to reduce their working hours as opposed to 29 percent who wished they could do so.

Case 2: Neil Walkingshaw
30 British mechanic Neil Walkingshaw was looking for a way to care for his newborn child in early 2000. **Reluctant** to hire a babysitter once his wife's maternity leave ended and she returned to work, Walkingshaw asked his employer if he could switch to part-time hours in order to spend half of each day at home looking after his son. His employer refused, saying the paperwork would be "too messy" and that it would be difficult to get anyone to share

35 Walkingshaw's job. Knowing that the company he worked for had granted similar requests to female employees, Walkingshaw **sued** on the grounds of sex **discrimination**. On November 20, 2001, an industrial court ruled that Walkingshaw had been discriminated against and awarded him £3,600. The ruling is believed to be the first of its kind, and demonstrates just how much views on parental roles have changed over the years.

40 It's probably safe to say that the stay-at-home dad is here to stay. As more and more pioneers like Masato Yamada and Neil Walkingshaw fight for **concessions** from their employers, they contribute immensely to the flexibility of the father's role in the modern family. There is still a stigma attached to stay-at-home dads in the working world. Some employers see "stay-at-home dad" as meaning "couldn't find work"; others might view them as out of touch or lacking
45 **dedication** to their career. However, many stay-at-home dads see children as a **priority** that is worth sacrificing for.

¹**conventional wisdom** traditional or usual view or opinion
²**sole** only
³**maternity leave** period of time after a woman has a child, usually three to six months, when she takes time off from work
⁴**paternity leave** by analogy with maternity leave, a period of time that a father takes off from work to take care of a new child

A Complete the sentences with information from the reading. Write no more than three words for each answer.

1 Having a father in the home helps to lower _____ among young people.
2 Many men wishing to become stay-at-home dads find opposition from _____.
3 Masato Yamada's boss's reaction to his request was, "_____?"
4 Neil Walkingshaw wanted to switch to _____ hours.
5 For some employers, "stay-at-home dad" means "_____."

B Choose the best answer for each question or statement about the reading. Try not to look back at the reading for the answers.

1 By the 1980s, more women were _____, and fewer men were _____.
   a. in the workplace / the main source of income
   b. having children / in the delivery room
   c. getting jobs / in the workplace
2 Which of the following is NOT true about Masato Yamada's story?
   a. His wife had taken maternity leave.
   b. He requested paternity leave.
   c. His boss was happy to help him.

3 Which of the following is NOT true about Walkingshaw's story?
   a. He sued his employer for unfair treatment.
   b. He had to pay a £3,600 fine.
   c. His employer allowed new mothers to work part-time.
4 According to the article, the "stay-at-home dad" is probably _____.
   a. a high-paying job   b. here to stay   c. a temporary trend

C Critical Thinking

Discuss these questions with a partner.
1 Why do you think Yamada's boss initially resisted his request for paternity leave?
2 The author reports that the absence of a father in the family is the single biggest social problem in modern society. Why do you think so?

Vocabulary Comprehension:
Words in Context

A The words in *italics* are vocabulary items from the reading. Read each question or statement and choose the correct answer. Compare your answers with a partner.

1 The *breadwinner* typically _____ money.
   a. earns   b. spends
2 If a company makes a *concession* in negotiation, they _____.
   a. push hard for something   b. give something up
3 A worker might show *dedication* to the company by _____.
   a. working all weekend   b. looking for another job
4 Which would be an example of *discrimination*?
   a. paying someone less money because of his or her age
   b. allowing parents to leave work early when a child is sick
5 A person _____ 18 is considered a *juvenile* in many countries.
   a. over   b. under
6 If something is a *priority*, it is _____.
   a. exciting   b. important
7 Jimmy is *reluctant* to dance because he is _____.
   a. a very shy person   b. a very talented dancer
8 My neighbor is going to *sue* me, so I have to _____.
   a. get a lawyer   b. call the police
9 A company is more likely to *reap* benefits by _____.
   a. being sued   b. having dedicated employees

B Answer these questions. Discuss your answers with a partner.

1 Who is the *breadwinner* of your family?
2 What is a *concession* that a company might make to angry workers?
3 How might someone show *dedication* to learning English?
4 In the past, in what ways have some companies shown *discrimination* to employees or customers?
5 When is a person no longer considered to be a *juvenile* in your country?
6 Right now in your life, what is your number one *priority*?
7 What should young people do to *reap* benefits when they are older?
8 What are some reasons a person might be *reluctant* to speak their second language?
9 For what reason might one person *sue* another?

A Study the words in the chart. What do you think they mean? Match each word with a definition below. Use your dictionary to help you.

Noun	Verb	Adjective
matriarch maternity	to mother	maternal
patriarch paternity	patronize to father	patriotic paternal
juvenile	rejuvenate	juvenile

Vocabulary Skill:
The Root Words *pater*, *mater*, and *juv*

In this chapter, you read the adjectives "juvenile" and "paternal." There are many words in English that begin with or include the root words "juv" meaning "young," "pater/patri" meaning "father," and "mater/matri" meaning "mother."

1 to talk down to someone, to speak to a person like a child _____
2 the female leader of a family, usually the oldest or wisest _____
3 motherhood or pregnancy _____
4 loyal to a country _____
5 to care for or nurture someone _____
6 to feel refreshed again, usually after a rest _____
7 related to fatherhood or being a father _____
8 young; can also mean childish or immature _____
9 the male leader of a family, usually the oldest or wisest _____
10 related to the mother _____

B Answer these questions. Then share your answers with a partner.

1 What is the name of your maternal grandmother?
2 How old is your paternal grandfather?
3 Give an example of juvenile behavior.
4 Is maternity leave common in your country? How much time off work do women usually take?
5 Talk about something that rejuvenates you.
6 Are you a patriotic person?
7 Is there a patriarch or matriarch in your family? Describe this person.

Real Life Skill:
Describing Family Relationships

In this unit, you've read about the changing family. In today's world, many people's families include more than their biological parents and siblings. There are some common names used to refer to these types of relatives.

A Look at the words and phrases below. Match each with a definition.

1 mother-in-law/father-in-law _____
2 ex-wife/ex-husband _____
3 step-brother/sister _____
4 half brother/sister _____
5 adopted _____
6 step-mother/step-father _____
7 step-son/step-daughter _____

a. another person's child legally made a member of your family
b. a sibling related to you by marriage only
c. your parent's spouse, but not your parent
d. a child related to you by marriage only
e. your spouse's parent
f. your former spouse
g. a sibling who shares the same mother or father as you

B Read the newspaper announcement below. Then use words from A to answer the questions. Be sure to use the correct form of the words.

Hollywood Couple Announces New Family Addition

Actor Nicole Sommers is expecting a baby girl with husband Miguel Santiago in May. Ms. Sommers has a daughter from a previous marriage, Michelle, age 7, now living with her father, director Cameron DuBois. Mr. Santiago has twin boys, Alberto and Jorge, age 10, who live with his ex-wife. Sommers and Santiago adopted a little girl three months ago named Angelina. Ms. Sommers is currently shooting her latest film in the south of Spain, where she is staying with her in-laws.

1 Miguel Santiago is Michelle's _____.
2 Alberto and Jorge are Michelle's _____.
3 The new baby will be Jorge and Alberto's _____.
4 Miguel Santiago's father is Ms. Sommers's _____.
5 Alberto and Jorge are Nicole Sommers's _____.
6 Cameron DuBois is Ms. Sommers's _____.
7 Angelina is Michelle, Alberto, and Jorge's _____.

What Do You Think?

1 If you have siblings, do you get along with them? Would you prefer to be an only child? If you are an only child, do you wish you had siblings?
2 Do you think men face any sort of social discrimination? Give an example.
3 In your country, do you think that men participate equally in child rearing?
4 Do you hope that stay-at-home dads become more common in the future? Why or why not?

Fluency Strategy: *SQ3R*

SQ3R will help you be a better, more fluent reader and increase your reading comprehension. SQ3R stands for **S**urvey, **Q**uestion, **R**ead, **R**eview, **R**ecite.

Survey

Survey is similar to the A in the ACTIVE approach to reading; **A**ctivate prior knowledge. When you survey, you prepare yourself by skimming quickly through the text you will read. You read the title, the headings, and the first sentence in each section of the passage. You look for and read words that are written in **bold** or *italics*. Look at any pictures and read any captions. Through the survey, you prepare yourself to read.

Look at "The Dangers of Dieting" on the next page. Read the title and the first sentence in each of the five paragraphs.

Question

After the survey, but before you read, ask yourself **questions**. "What do I want to learn as I read?"

Based on your survey of "The Dangers of Dieting," write two or three questions that you hope to answer as you read.

1 _____

2 _____

3 _____

Read

Following the survey and question stages of SQ3R, you **read**. You focus on comprehending the material. You move your eyes fluently through the material.

Read "The Dangers of Dieting." As you read, keep in mind the 12 tips on pages 8 and 9. By combining those tips and SQ3R you will improve your reading fluency.

The Dangers of Dieting

Thanks to our modern lifestyle, with more and more time spent sitting down in front of computers than ever before, the number of overweight people is at a new high. As people frantically search for a solution to this problem, they often try some of the popular fad diets being offered. Many people see fad diets as innocuous ways of losing weight, and they are grateful to have them. Unfortunately, not only don't fad
5 diets usually do the trick, they can actually be dangerous for your health.

Although permanent weight loss is the goal, few are able to achieve it. Experts estimate that 95 percent of dieters return to their starting weight, or even add weight. While the reckless use of fad diets can bring some initial results, long-term results are very rare.

10 Nonetheless, people who are fed up with the difficulties of changing their eating habits often turn to fad diets. Rather than being moderate, fad diets involve extreme dietary changes. They advise eating only one type of food, or they prohibit other types of foods entirely. This results in a situation where a person's body doesn't get all the vitamins and other things that it needs to stay healthy.

15 One popular fad diet recommends eating lots of meat and animal products, while nearly eliminating carbohydrates. A scientific study from Britain found that this diet is very high in fat. According to the study, the increase of damaging fats in the blood can lead to heart disease and, in extreme cases, kidney failure. Furthermore, diets that are too low in carbohydrates can cause the body to use its own muscle for energy. The less muscle you have, the less food you use up, and the result is slower weight loss.

20 Veteran dieters may well ask at this point, "What is the ideal diet?" Well, to some extent, it depends on the individual. A United States government agency has determined that to change your eating habits requires changing your psychology of eating, and everyone has a different psychology. That being said, the British study quoted above recommends a diet that is high in carbohydrates and high in fiber, with portions of fatty foods kept low. According to the study, such a diet is the best for people who want to
25 stay healthy, lose weight, and keep that weight off. And, any dieting program is best undertaken with a doctor's supervision.

Review

After you read, you **review**. During the review stage of SQ3R you review the questions that you asked yourself prior to reading.

Did you find answers to your questions? Write the answers below.

1 _____

2 _____

3 _____

Recite

The final step of SQ3R is to **recite** what you have learned while reading. The important thing is that you close your book and remember what you have read. You can recite in different ways.

- **If you are alone, write down the key information that you learned as you were reading.**
- **If you have a partner, talk to him or her about what you have read.**

1 What is the author's main point?
   a. Reckless fad dieting probably takes weight off the fastest.
   b. Most people shouldn't try to lose weight.
   c. High-protein diets can make you sick.
   d. Fad diets are ineffective and unsafe; high-carbohydrate, low-fat diets are best.

2 According to the passage, why are there more overweight people nowadays?
   a. They are using fad diets.
   b. They spend a lot of time in front of computers.
   c. They have heart disease.
   d. They are eating more protein than ever before.

3 After losing weight by dieting, what usually happens to people?
   a. They have kidney failure.
   b. They gain the weight back again.
   c. They keep the weight off.
   d. They have less muscle.

4 Which of the following best expresses the essential information in paragraph 3?
   a. Fed up people turn to fad diets, which, being too extreme, don't give the body everything it needs.
   b. People are fed up with fad diets and turn to diets which provide what the body needs.
   c. People prefer fad dieting to moderate dieting because it requires fewer foods to give the body what it needs.
   d. Fad diets give fed up people the moderate dietary changes they need to get all the required vitamins.

5 Which is not mentioned as an effect of the meat and animal product diet?
   a. heart disease
   b. slower weight loss
   c. psychological changes
   d. kidney failure

6 According to the passage, why does the ideal diet depend on the individual?
   a. The less muscle you have, the less food you use up.
   b. Everyone can gain the weight back.
   c. Everyone has a different psychology.
   d. Everyone likes different foods.

7 According to the passage, what diet does a British study recommend?
   a. a meat and animal product diet
   b. a diet high in carbohydrates, low in fiber, and high in fat
   c. a fad diet but with healthier foods
   d. a diet high in carbohydrates, high in fiber, and low in fat

Self Check

Write a short answer to each of the following questions.

1. Have you ever used the SQ3R method before?

   Yes   No   *I'm not sure.*

2. Do you think SQ3R is helpful? Why or why not?

   _____

3. Will you practice SQ3R in your reading outside of English class?

   _____

   _____

4. Which of the six reading passages in units 7–9 did you enjoy most? Why?

   _____

   _____

5. Which of the six reading passages in units 7–9 was easiest? Which was most difficult? Why?

   _____

   _____

6. What have you read in English outside of class recently?

   _____

   _____

7. What distractions do you face when you read? What can you do to minimize those distractions?

   _____

   _____

8. How will you try to improve your reading fluency from now on?

   _____

Review Reading 5: *Space Travel and Science Fiction*

Fluency Practice

Time yourself as you read through the passage. Try to read as fluently as you can. Record your time in the Reading Rate Chart on page 208. Then answer the questions on the following page.

Space Travel and Science Fiction

Space travel and science fiction have long been connected. Early science fiction writers such as Jules Verne inspired scientists and engineers to develop new space technologies. Writers of science fiction,
5 as well as creators of science fiction TV shows and movies, often study the latest scientific concepts and use or adapt them to help portray what future space travel, space ships, and space stations might look like. And while many of their predictions have come
10 true, many others have not.

Jules Verne (1828–1905) was a French author. He was a pioneer of science fiction. In his novels *From the Earth to the Moon* (1865) and *Around the Moon* (1870), a kind of space ship is fired from a 900-foot-
15 long cannon at the moon. On their journey, the three travelers are deprived of gravity at one point and float around their small ship. When landing on the moon, rockets are used to slow the ship down.

Given the year in which he was writing, Verne's
20 predictions were very good. The size of his space ship is about the size of the first one to go to the moon, the *Apollo*, minus its large rockets. Both Verne's ship and the *Apollo* carried three people into space. Furthermore, rockets were indeed used by the *Apollo* to slow its descent. However, Verne's ship, by analogy with a gun, shot his travelers into space, which never could have worked. The
25 intense pressure of such an event would cause great physiological damage to the crew.

During the first half of the 20th century, science fiction novels and comic books were widely distributed in the United States. Their portrayal of space travel was less far-fetched than Verne's. Pictures began showing astronauts in space suits, as writers realized that exposure of human beings to space was deadly. Ideas of other planets were still often wrong, though. A 1928 drawing
30 of the surface of a moon of the planet Jupiter shows it covered in plant life. Only later was it discovered that other than Earth, the planets and moons around our sun are without life as we know it.

Drawings in the early 20th century showed very large space ships and stations. They were like floating cities. Writers at the time knew that trips to other stars would take hundreds of years. Those who left Earth would die on the journey; their descendants would arrive. Some writers avoided this
35 problem by using the concept of suspended animation—a deep sleep in which a person doesn't grow older. Such travelers would awaken at the end of their journey, hundreds of years in the future. It is not impossible that these ideas could become reality one day.

After the American space program had begun, the television show *Star Trek* became very popular. It follows the adventures of a large space ship with over 400 crew members that flies around the
40 universe at speeds faster than light. This is a wonderful dream, but it will probably never come to fulfillment. The laws of physics tell us that it is quite impossible for any object to travel faster than the speed of light.

It's clear to see that science fiction has progressed along with science and technology. Science fiction writers continue to study scientific concepts and to use them to portray the future. Looking
45 back at their ideas, some were correct and cannot be distinguished from today's reality; many others were nothing but fiction. But, they have always inspired new generations of humans to dream of someday going into space.

591 words   Time taken _____

Reading Comprehension

1 Which of the following best summarizes the author's main idea?
 a. The inspiring ideas of science fiction writers have been both right and wrong about the future of space travel.
 b. Though often correct, the incorrect ideas of science fiction writers have caused scientists and engineers to make mistakes.
 c. Science fiction writers make inspiring, incorrect predictions about what scientists and engineers will do next.
 d. Scientists and engineers create inspiring science fiction that usually comes true.

2 Which of the following predictions by Jules Verne was incorrect?
 a. The first space ship would carry a crew of three people.
 b. Space travelers would be deprived of gravity.
 c. Rockets would be used to slow down a space ship.
 d. A space ship would be launched using the analogy of a gun.

3 According to the passage, which statement about 20th century science fiction is NOT true?
 a. It showed space stations like floating cities.
 b. It showed astronauts in space suits.
 c. It showed plant life on a moon of Jupiter.
 d. It discovered ways in which objects can travel faster than light.

4 According to the passage, what was the purpose of a very large space ship?
 a. It flew to other stars much more quickly.
 b. It held enough fuel for the centuries-long journey to other stars.
 c. For centuries-long trips, people would have families and their descendants would arrive.
 d. It was a place for humans to escape to if Earth was destroyed.

5 According to the passage, suspended animation was a concept used in science fiction to _____.
 a. allow people to travel for hundreds of years
 b. help sick people wait for their disease to be cured
 c. help people wait for descendants to arrive at another planet
 d. get a lot of rest on centuries-long journeys

6 In line 40, what does the phrase "a wonderful dream" refer to?
 a. the American space program
 b. the television show *Star Trek*
 c. a space ship with more than 400 crew members
 d. traveling faster than the speed of light

7 Why can't human beings travel faster than the speed of light?
 a. Our space ships are too large.
 b. The rockets we can currently produce are too weak.
 c. It's against the laws of physics.
 d. It would cause too much physiological damage to the crew.

Fluency Practice

Time yourself as you read through the passage. Try to read as fluently as you can. Record your time in the Reading Rate Chart on page 208. Then answer the questions on the following page..

Single-Parent Families: Changing Views

In the opinion of many people, the two-parent family is the correct way to raise children. Historically, this has been seen as the most natural way, and in the past,
5 single-parent families have had to deal with the stigma attached to their lifestyle. Nowadays, however, the single-parent family is the fastest growing type of family. Single parenthood can be the
10 result of the death, divorce, separation, or abandonment of one parent, but also of single-parent adoption or scientific fertility methods allowing a woman to have a child on her own. In the United States, a
15 national survey showed that at least 50 percent of children, at some point in their childhood, will be members of a single-parent home. Therefore, we need to make it a priority to leave the stigma behind and
20 to see the strengths of the single-parent home.

Whether they elect to be single parents or are given no choice, single parents are usually at a disadvantage in many ways when compared to two-parent families. In a family with only one breadwinner, money is often in short supply. Compared to homes
25 where one parent is wholly dedicated to child rearing, children receive less attention. Parents can find themselves overwhelmed by their responsibilities both at work and at home.

Despite these disadvantages, it is possible for single-parent families to do well. Single parents must look for support groups and understanding friends that help them keep their self-esteem high. They need to remember that nobody does it alone, and that today's single parents use social networks to make up for their disadvantages. Quality schools and community and religious organizations are examples of these.

Surprisingly, single-parent families also have certain advantages over two-parent families. Single parents have greater flexibility in spending time with children, because they don't have to take the needs and schedule of a husband or wife into consideration. Another advantage comes from the fact that single parents naturally work together with their children to solve problems. This give-and-take between parents and children, and children and their siblings, as they negotiate important life decisions makes children feel more needed and valued.

It's important to mention the special challenges faced by the single father. Even today, when the social roles of males and females are less clear than years ago, many people are reluctant to admit that men can be effective single parents. Nonetheless, cooking, cleaning, and shopping are not particularly difficult for single fathers. And they also report developing closer relationships with their children. Single fathers also show more interest in the education and protection of their children.

Children of single parents have to fight against some frightening statistics. They seem to show that these children's chances of becoming juvenile criminals are higher than normal. Other statistics claim that these children are more likely to drop out of school in their teens and to be jobless in their early 20s. A connection has even been made between children of single parents and higher rates of being overweight and using illegal drugs. It must be conceded that such statistics are indeed worrying. Nonetheless, it's important to remember that single-parent homes have, until now, suffered discrimination from a world that considered them unsatisfactory. As single-parent families start getting the community support they need and become more accepted by society, this situation is certain to improve. In the future we will likely see these statistics disappear.

There is no denying the difficulties of the single-parent home. Overcoming these challenges is hard work for single parents. But, with the support from friends and the community, single parents and their children can reap the satisfying rewards of watching their children grow up to be happy and healthy.

620 words   Time taken _____

Reading Comprehension

1 Which statement about single-parent families would the author most likely agree with?
   a. They are better than two-parent families.
   b. They are unnatural and harmful to children.
   c. They require extra support from the community.
   d. They are probably the best lifestyle for raising children.

2 According to the first paragraph, why is it important that we leave behind the stigma attached to single-parent families?
   a. because scientific fertility methods are growing
   b. because the number of single-parent families is growing fast
   c. because many people don't see them as correct
   d. because single parenthood can be the result of divorce

3 Which is NOT a disadvantage of single-parent families as compared to two-parent families?
   a. Sometimes there isn't as much money.
   b. Children can receive less attention.
   c. Parents can be overwhelmed by their responsibilities.
   d. Children do not feel valued.

4 According to the passage, what can single parents do to keep their self-esteem high?
   a. get married
   b. make time for themselves away from children
   c. find support groups and understanding friends
   d. dress their children in brand-name clothing

5 According to the passage, in which way can a single-parent home have an advantage over a two-parent home?
   a. Because they are more involved in problem solving, the children can feel more needed and valued.
   b. Without two parents to control them, children grow up more naturally.
   c. Single parents make more decisions for their children, so they make fewer mistakes.
   d. Working single parents can train their children for a future career.

6 According to the passage, which of the following is a difficulty for single fathers?
   a. cooking
   b. cleaning
   c. shopping
   d. none of the above

7 Why does the author believe that the negative statistics about children of single-parent homes will disappear in the future?
   a. There will be fewer and fewer single-parent families.
   b. Single-parent families will become more fully accepted by society.
   c. People will understand that there is a stigma attached to single-parent families.
   d. Single parents will work much harder to educate and control their children.

Getting Ready

For items 1–8, check (✔) the statement you most agree with. Then, discuss your answers with a partner.

PUBLIC EDUCATION SURVEY

1   **a.** Government spending on education should be increased. _____
     b. The government already spends enough on education. _____

2   **a.** Public education would improve if parents were more involved with their children's education. _____
     b. Educating children is the teacher's responsibility; parents needn't concern themselves with it. _____

3   **a.** Strict discipline in public schools has a negative effect on the quality of education. _____
     b. Strict discipline improves the educational experience of middle and high school students. _____

4   **a.** Standardized testing is the best way to measure student success. _____
     b. Schools rely too heavily on tests to measure student success. _____
     c. Class work and homework are better methods than tests to measure student success. _____

5   **a.** Privately owned schools are generally better than public schools. _____
     b. Public schools are generally superior to privately owned schools. _____

6   **a.** All middle and high school teachers should have higher degrees in the subjects they teach. _____
     b. A general education degree is a sufficient foundation for teaching any subject in public middle and high schools. _____

7   **a.** All public schools offer a similar level of education. _____
     b. Public schools in wealthier areas are better than those in poorer areas. _____

8   **a.** Too many activities in public schools distract students from their work. _____
     b. Public schools offer activities that are just as important to a child's education as classes. _____

Chapter 1: Homeschooling— A Better Way to Learn?

Before You Read:
School Days

A Discuss these questions with a partner.

1 What schools have you attended?
2 What are your positive memories of your school days?
3 What negative memories of school days do you have?
4 What choices do students have other than attending public high school?

Reading Skill:
Arguing For and Against a Topic

B What do you think about homeschooling—parents teaching their children at home rather than sending them to school? Discuss the following questions with a partner.

1 Is homeschooling allowed in your country?
2 Would you have preferred to be educated at home rather than at school?
3 What do you think the benefits of homeschooling are?
4 What could be some of the drawbacks of homeschooling?

Many reading passages present two sides of an argument—one argues for the topic; the other argues against it. Phrases such as "advocates of" and "in favor of" signal that information that supports the topic will be introduced. Phrases such as "critics of" or "concerns about" signal that information against the topic is coming. Also, words and phrases such as "but," "however," "though," "in contrast," and "in spite of" signal that an opposite or different opinion is about to be introduced.

A Read the passage and write down information from the reading.

Reasons For Homeschooling

1 _____
2 _____
3 _____
4 _____
5 _____
6 _____

Reasons Against Homeschooling

1 _____
2 _____
3 _____

B Compare your answers with a partner.

C Now read the passage again, then answer the questions that follow.

Homeschooling—A Better Way to Learn?

It is easy to forget that the public education system is a relatively new phenomenon. In fact, compulsory public education has only been in place for the past two centuries. Before that, while the affluent were able to hire tutors for their children, most education of children took place within the family and the community. In many countries where parents are looking for alternatives to the public education system, homeschooling is a growing trend.

Homeschooling is still considered to be a **radical** choice in most countries. The laws that apply to it can be complex and vary widely from country to country. In some countries, such as France, England, Taiwan, and the United States, homeschooling is permitted by law. In other countries, laws are not so clear, so homeschooling goes on but isn't formally permitted by existing laws. A third group of countries including Germany and Brazil prohibits homeschooling.

At one time, there was a stigma associated with homeschooling; it was traditionally used for students who could not attend school because of behavioral or learning difficulties. Today, however, more parents are taking on the responsibility of educating their children at home due to dissatisfaction with the educational system. Many parents are unhappy about class size, as well as problems inside the classroom. Teacher shortages and lack of funding mean that, in many schools, one teacher is responsible for 30 or 40 pupils. The result is often that children are deprived of the attention they need. **Escalating** classroom violence has also **motivated** some parents to remove their children from school. Advocates[1] of homeschooling believe that children learn better when they are in a **secure**, loving environment. They point out that homeschooled children reportedly do just as well as those who have been in the classroom, and many walk the campuses of top universities alongside the conventionally educated. Many psychologists see the home as the most natural learning environment. Parents who homeschool argue that they can monitor their children's education and give them the attention that is lacking in a traditional school setting. Students can also pick and choose what to study and when to study, thus enabling them to learn at their own pace.

In contrast, critics of homeschooling say that children who are not in the classroom **miss out on** learning important social skills because they have little **interaction** with their peers. Many critics of homeschooling have raised concerns about the ability of parents to teach their kids effectively. Many parents who homeschool have no teacher training and are not **competent** educators of all the subjects taught in schools.

With an increasing number of **disgruntled** parents taking their children out of class, many school officials are looking for ways to **restore** parents' confidence in the public education system. Some schools in the United States have opened their doors to homeschoolers on a part-time basis, allowing these children to attend classes once or twice a week, or to take part in extracurricular activities[2] such as playing football or

taking ballet lessons. While many parents will not completely put their confidence back into the system,
40 many of them have reached a compromise that allows their children the extra benefits of peer interaction
and access to a wider choice of activities.

Whatever the arguments for or against it, homeschooling has become big business, and it is growing.
There are now websites, support groups, and conventions[3] that help parents to assert their rights and
enable them to learn more about educating their children. Though once the last resort[4] for troubled children,
45 homeschooling today is becoming an accepted alternative to the public educational system.

[1]**advocate** a person who believes in something and strongly supports and promotes it
[2]**extracurricular activities** extra activities done after class, usually for fun, but also for study
[3]**convention** a very large meeting, often of thousands of people who share the same interests or occupation
[4]**the last resort** the only choice remaining because everything else has failed

Reading Comprehension:

Check Your Understanding

A Choose the best answer for each question or statement about the reading below. Try not to look back at the reading for the answers.

1 The author wrote this passage in order to _____.
   a. expose homeschooling as a threat to public education
   b. show that homeschooling is superior to a public school education
   c. give some background and explain people's opinions on the growing trend of homeschooling

2 Up until about 200 years ago, there was no _____.
   a. homeschooling   **b.** education   **c.** public school system

3 Which is not a reason cited by homeschooling advocates?
   a. class size   **b.** school sports   **c.** school violence

4 Some homeschooled children are returning to traditional schools part-time in order to participate in _____.
   a. football and ballet   **b.** math tests   **c.** teacher meetings

B Decide whether the following statements about the reading are true (T) or false (F). If you check (✔) false, correct the statement to make it true.

		T	F
1	There was a time when homeschooling was associated with learning disabilities.		
2	Homeschooled students are unable to get into the best universities.		
3	Critics of homeschooling say that children learn best in a loving environment.		
4	School officials are looking for ways to attract homeschoolers back to public schools.		
5	There are websites dedicated to teaching parents how to homeschool their children.		

C Critical Thinking

Discuss these questions with a partner.

1 Why do you think homeschooling is illegal in countries like Germany and Brazil?

2 What would you have missed the most about school if you had been homeschooled?

Vocabulary Comprehension:
Definition Matching

A Look at the list of words and phrases from the reading. Match each with a definition on the right.

1 competent _____

2 disgruntled _____

3 escalate _____

4 interaction _____

5 miss out on _____

6 motivated _____

7 radical _____

8 restore _____

9 secure _____

a. to bring something back to the way it was

b. capable, knowledgeable, or experienced

c. increase, usually in a negative or dangerous way

d. extreme

e. safe and protected

f. unhappy or displeased with something, often used to describe a person

g. to lose or not have a chance to do something that is fun or interesting

h. driven by a strong desire to do something

i. two things affecting each other

B Complete the sentences below using the vocabulary from A. Be sure to use the correct form of the word.

1 For the entire duration of parents' weekend, _____ between parents and teachers is encouraged.

2 I'm grateful that our school has only _____, veteran teachers who know their subjects very well.

3 Hurry up and get up or you'll _____ breakfast!

4 This taxi driver is too reckless. I don't feel _____ in this cab.

5 Most of the employees don't like the supervisor, and they are becoming more and more _____ every day.

6 Of all the ways to lose weight, surgery is the most _____ way.

7 Historians and archeologists have undertaken a project to _____ the great temple to its initial condition.

8 Ji-young is very _____ to succeed in business, so she works long hours every day.

9 Experts are worried that _____ inflation may cause prices of food to increase again this month.

Vocabulary Skill:

The Root Word
ven/vent

In this chapter you read the adverb "conventionally," meaning "usually" or "traditionally," and the noun form "convention," meaning "a large meeting of people." Both words include the root word "ven," meaning "to come." "Ven," sometimes also written as "vent," is combined with prefixes and suffixes to form many English words.

A For each word, study the different parts. Then, write its part of speech and a simple definition. Use your dictionary to help you. Share your ideas with a partner.

Vocabulary	Part of Speech	Definition
1 conventional	adjective	usual or traditional
2 convene		
3 circumvent		
4 intervene		
5 inventory		
6 revenue		
7 prevention		

B Complete each sentence using words from the chart. Be sure to use the correct form of the word.

1 The key to staying healthy is _____—don't smoke, don't drink too much, and try to visit your doctor once a year for a full health check.

2 A large crowd _____ in front of the university to hear the president speak.

3 Before Carl could hit Scott, Brett _____ and stopped the fight.

4 Thanks to a great sales team, the company has almost doubled its _____ this year.

5 In the United States, cigarette companies can't advertise on TV. However, many of these companies _____ this rule by advertising at sporting events that are televised.

6 I'm afraid we don't have any more of Yo-Yo Ma's CDs in our _____, but I can order a copy of his latest release if you like.

C Can you think of any other words in English that include the root *ven/vent*?

Chapter 2: Suggestopedia

Unit 10

Before You Read:
Speeding Up Your Learning

A Some people claim that the following strategies can speed up language learning. Check (✔) any that you use.

1 I study languages in a comfortable location. _____
2 I use music to help me learn. _____
3 I use memory techniques to remember more vocabulary. _____
4 I join study groups. _____
5 I use videos, tapes, radio, etc., to help me learn. _____
6 I try to relax my mind before starting to learn. _____
7 I keep a vocabulary notebook with words and pictures or charts. _____

B Discuss the strategies in A with a partner. What other strategies do you think are effective for learning languages?

Reading Skill:
Identifying Meaning from Content

> To guess the meaning of an important but unfamiliar word in a reading passage, try the following: First, think about how the new word is related to the topic of the reading. Second, identify what part of speech the word is. Third, look at the words surrounding the new word for synonyms, antonyms, or an explanation of the word.

A Read the sentences below. Which sentence best helps you to understand the meaning of the word "inhibition"? Explain your answer to a partner.

1 He has inhibitions.
2 He has inhibitions that hold him back.
3 He has inhibitions in his mind that hold him back from doing the things he wants to do.

B Find each italicized word in the reading below. Read the sentence in which the word appears and some of the surrounding sentences. Then choose the best definition.

1 In line 22, the word *suggestible* probably means _____.
   a. able to suggest   **b.** easy to influence   **c.** ready to make suggestions
2 In line 36, the word *intonation* probably means _____.
   a. use of the voice   **b.** wording   **c.** presentation
3 In line 39, the word *reciting* probably means _____.
   a. writing   **b.** speaking publicly   **c.** imagining
4 In line 43, the word *elaboration* probably means _____.
   a. expanding in detail   **b.** production   **c.** enjoyment

C Read through the reading passage again, then answer the questions that follow.

Suggestopedia

Dr. Georgi Lozanov

Suggestopedia is the name for a language teaching methodology[1] developed in the 1970s by the Bulgarian psychologist Georgi Lozanov. The term comes from the words *suggest* and *pedagogy*, or teaching. The methodology
5 rests on the belief that people have great mental abilities that they don't ordinarily use. However, under the right conditions these abilities can be opened up and people can learn great amounts of new material. The key to opening up people's mental powers lies in achieving the right mental **state**—that
10 is, they need to feel happy, relaxed, and open to new experiences. In 1964 Lozanov conducted a famous experiment with 14 language students at the University of Sofia to prove this point. According to the published results, the students were able to memorize 1,000 new French words at 90 to 100 percent accuracy in a single session.

15 For students to achieve the ideal mental state for learning, they must be both physically and emotionally relaxed. Physical relaxation is provided by comfortable seating and an attractive environment. The teacher has an important function in helping students to relax emotionally. The teacher's positive attitude makes students feel that they **are bound to** succeed. Since the suggestopedia-trained teacher joins playfully in many activities and never criticizes a student, he
20 or she is seen more as a friend. But, the teacher's role as an authority is also important to learning. Why? Because students are more likely to remember information that comes from someone they consider an expert. In a sense, for students to become **suggestible**, it helps if they look upon the teacher as a parent and themselves as a child.

Because it affects people's moods so strongly, music plays an important role in suggestopedia.
25 Lozanov says that Baroque music by composers such as Mozart, Vivaldi, and Handel is ideal for achieving the right mood for learning. He points to research which shows that Baroque music both relaxes the body and activates the brain, and recommends that students listen to Baroque music at various points in the lesson.

The standard suggestopedia lesson has a four-part structure:

Introduction
30 The main purpose at this stage is to relax students and get them in the mood for learning. Students are encouraged to adopt the name and identity of a native speaker of the new language. This helps them to free themselves from their usual **inhibitions**.

Concert
35 The concert stage has two **phases**: active and passive. In the first or active phase, the teacher reads a piece of text slowly with dramatic **intonation**. The text could be part of a play, a poem, or a

short reading. The piece is translated into the students' native language so that they can read and think about the meaning while the teacher is speaking. Certain words are repeated several times, and the students may join in **reciting** the text aloud. During this phase the students begin to pick up bits of grammar and vocabulary. After a break, the passive phase begins. The teacher reads the text at normal speed with natural intonation. Students listen quietly while music plays softly in the background.

Elaboration

In the **elaboration** phase, students participate in many types of activities that help them learn the language that was introduced earlier.

Production

In this final stage students are encouraged to ask questions and to use the language in a free and creative manner.

People have criticized suggestopedia on several grounds. For example, some have said that the methodology rests on unproven assumptions and that Lozanov's students could not possibly have learned as much or as fast as he claimed. Still, language teachers have found some of suggestopedia's techniques useful. The movement has also **given rise to** two successful and widely used teaching methodologies called "accelerated learning" and "superlearning."

¹**methodology** a system of methods, rules, and ideas for doing something

---

A **Choose the best answer for each question or statement about the reading. Try not to look back at the reading for the answers.**

1 The author's purpose in this passage is to _____ suggestopedia.
   a. promote   **b.** warn people about   **c.** explain
2 Lozanov's 1964 suggestopedia experiment with 14 students was _____.
   a. successful   **b.** a failure   **c.** unplanned
3 In suggestopedia, it's useful for the student to look on the teacher as _____.
   a. a professional   **b.** a parent   **c.** another student
4 What are the two phases of the concert stage?
   a. fast and slow   **b.** grammar and vocabulary   **c.** active and passive

B **Complete the sentences with information from the reading. Write no more than three words for each answer.**

1 In suggestopedia, students are most ready to learn when they are both physically and emotionally _____.
2 The four stages of a suggestopedia lesson are introduction, concert, _____.
3 According to Lozanov, Baroque music relaxes the body and activates _____.
4 In the introduction stage, the students adopt _____ and identity of a native speaker of the new language.
5 Suggestopedia has been criticized as relying on _____.

Reading Comprehension:
Check Your Understanding

C Critical Thinking

Discuss these questions with a partner.

1 Why do you suppose suggestopedia isn't used in more classrooms?
2 What other language-learning methods or schools do you know?
3 If you were asked to learn 1,000 words, how would you go about learning them?

Vocabulary Comprehension:
Words in Context

A **The words in *italics* are vocabulary items from the reading. Read each question or statement and choose the correct answer. Check your answers with a partner.**

1 Our dog *is bound to* have more physiological ailments _____.
   a. as it gets older   **b.** when we travel with it
2 When you *elaborate*, you _____.
   a. give more details   **b.** speak generally about something
3 Humans' harnessing of atomic power *gave rise to* _____.
   a. nuclear power   **b.** years of research
4 Siblings can be very different. While I'm always wrestling with *inhibitions*, my brother _____.
   a. is as free as a bird   **b.** always thinks before he acts
5 Rising *intonation* at the end of a sentence usually indicates _____.
   a. a question   **b.** a statement
6 If a project occurs in *phases*, then it _____.
   a. increases over time   **b.** happens in a series of steps
7 The teacher asked Malcolm to *recite* the poem, so he _____.
   a. copied it down   **b.** read it for the class
8 New university students are often in a *state* of _____.
   a. confusion   **b.** the dormitories
9 Kayla is so *suggestible* that she will do anything that _____.
   a. she wants to do   **b.** anyone advises her to do

B **Answer these questions. Discuss your answers with a partner.**

1 Who are some people you *are bound to* meet every week?
2 What new businesses did the Internet *give rise to*?
3 What can you do to lessen your *inhibitions* about speaking a foreign language?
4 How is the *intonation* of your native language different from that of English?
5 Can you *elaborate* on your plans for this weekend?
6 What are some of the different *phases* of the moon?
7 Which poems can you *recite* from memory?
8 What is your favorite *state* of mind to be in?
9 Whom do you know who is *suggestible*?

A Read these rules regarding the formation of adjectives with *-ible* and *-able*.

1 If the root word is a complete word, add *-able*.
comfort + able = comfortable   laugh + able = laughable

2 If the root word is a complete word ending in *-e*, drop the final *-e* and add *-able*.
value + able = valuable   desire + able = desirable

3 If the root word is a complete word ending in *-y*, change *-y* to *-i* and add *-able*.
rely + able = reliable   deny + able = deniable

4 If the root word is not a complete word, add *-ible*.
vis + ible = visible   terr + ible = terrible

Exceptions to these rules include: *flexible, responsible, irritable, digestible, inevitable, negotiable*.

B Use the rules to create the *-able* or *-ible* forms of the words below.

Word or Root	-able or -ible form
adore	
wash	
poss	
incred	
elect	
remark	
suit	
elig	
profit	
avail	
restore	
sens	

C Complete the sentences with a word ending in *-able* or *-ible* from A or B. Sometimes more than one answer is possible.

1 The furniture repair store told me that, because of long exposure to the sun, the color of this sofa isn't _____.

2 That actor's portrayal of Abraham Lincoln in that movie was truly _____.

3 Beatrice's little brother is a brat, but her little sister is _____.

4 Ten-year-old Mark's juvenile attempts to act grown up were quite _____.

5 The family breadwinner, my father, has never missed a day of work in his life. He is a very _____ person.

6 A politician must be popular to be _____.

7 Deprived of his teddy bear, Joshua couldn't get _____ in his bed.

8 They were reluctant to close down a business that had been so _____.

Vocabulary Skill:
The Suffixes *-ible* and *-able*

In this chapter you learned the word "suggestible," which ends with the suffix "-ible." The suffixes "-ible" and "-able" can mean "able to be" or "fit to be," or express capacity or worthiness in general. There are many more words that are formed with "-able," but it is difficult to say comprehensively which words take "-ible" and which take "-able" as there are many exceptions to the rule, but there are a number of helpful rules that cover the majority of cases.

A **Practice saying each abbreviation. Then, match each abbreviation with the correct phrase.**

Degree		Definition	
1	B.A. _____	a	Master of Science
2	B.S. _____	b	Master of Arts
3	A.A. _____	c	Bachelor of Science
4	M.A. _____	d	Doctor of Philosophy
5	M.S. _____	e	Master of Business Administration
6	M.Ed. _____	f	Bachelor of Arts
7	M.B.A. _____	g	Associate of Arts
8	Ph.D. _____	h	Master of Education

There are many common abbreviations used to refer to qualifications, or academic degrees, one receives after a period of study. These abbreviations are written as well as said, and when spoken, each letter of the abbreviation is usually pronounced.

B **Write the appropriate abbreviation next to each description. Check your answers with a partner.**

A person who graduates from a . . .	has a(n)
1 university with a degree in biology	
2 two-year junior, or community, college	
3 university with a higher degree in history, one level above a bachelor's	
4 university with a degree in English	
5 university with a degree in business, one level above a bachelor's	
6 university with a degree in engineering, one level above a bachelor's	
7 university with a degree of the highest rank, above a master's	
8 university or college with a degree in education, one level above a bachelor's	

What Do You Think?

1 Up to what age is education compulsory in your country?
2 Up to this point in your life, do you think you've received a good education or not? Explain your answer.
3 What kind of formal education must a person have in order to become a teacher in your country?
4 If you could make changes to the educational system in your country, what would you change and why?

Complete the survey below. Compare your answers with a partner.

Memory Survey

	Yes	No
1 Do you ever have trouble remembering people's names?	☐	☐
2 Do you ever forget important dates such as birthdays and anniversaries?	☐	☐
3 Do you remember what you did on your last birthday?	☐	☐
How about on the day before that?	☐	☐
4 Do you often forget where you put things?	☐	☐
5 Do you ever forget to pay bills?	☐	☐
6 Can you remember the last three movies you saw? Write them down.	☐	☐

a. _____

b. _____

c. _____

7 Can you remember the names of the last three novels you read? ☐ ☐

Write them down.

a. _____

b. _____

c. _____

8 Do you remember what you studied in your last English class? ☐ ☐

If yes, what? _____

Based on your answers to the questions above, do you think you have a good or bad memory? Explain your answer.

Chapter 1: How Good Is Your Memory?

Before You Read:
Predicting Content

A There are four subtitled paragraphs in the reading passage. Without reading them, try to predict what information you will find, and write down your ideas.

1 The Hippocampus _____

2 Creating Memories _____

3 Memory Loss _____

4 Improving Memory _____

B Compare your ideas with a partner.

C Match the words and phrases on the left with the definitions on the right.

1 via _____   **a.** sight, hearing, taste, smell, touch

2 senses _____ **b.** a disease of the brain resulting in forgetfulness

3 stimuli _____ **c.** a part of the brain

4 neurons _____ **d.** to follow a path or trail of evidence to find something

5 cerebral cortex _____ **e.** the creation of new brain cells

6 Alzheimer's _____ **f.** brain cells

7 neurogenesis _____ **g.** things that excite activity or attention

8 trace _____ **h.** through; by way of; by means of

Reading Skill:
Skimming for the Main Idea

Skimming is one way to look for the main ideas in a reading. When we skim, we read over parts of the text very quickly. We don't need to read every word or look up words we don't understand; we just need to get a general idea of what something is about. This can save time when an understanding of details isn't required.

A Skim the reading passage quickly. Notice the title, subheads, photo, and any other interesting information.

B What is this reading mainly about?

1 parts of the brain that store information

2 illnesses that result in severe memory loss

3 how humans process, store, and recall information

C Read through the passage again, then answer the questions that follow.

How Good Is Your Memory?

Some people have **extraordinary** memories. According to the Guinness World Records,™ 2001, Gert Mittring of Germany can look at a list of 27 numbers for just four seconds and remember all of them. Most people, though, have trouble at times remembering where they put their door keys, or recalling the names of people they've recently met for the first time.

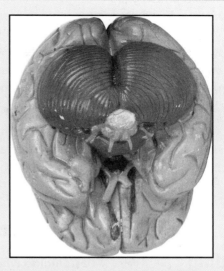

The Hippocampus

The process by which we store and **retrieve** information in our brains has been the focus of scientific research for many years. The brain is a highly complex organ that is not fully understood, and theories about how it works remain a topic of debate. It is generally agreed, though, that one area of the brain known as the hippocampus—named after the Latin word for "seahorse" because of its curved shape—is important in the process of recalling information. When we experience something, the information is sent via our senses to the hippocampus, where it is processed.

Creating Memories

Although the process of creating memories is only partially understood, it is thought to involve three main steps. Scientists believe that brain cells called neurons first **transform** the sensory stimuli we experience into images in our immediate memory. Then, these images are sent to the hippocampus and stored temporarily in short-term memory. In the hippocampus information is organized, and it is during this process that parts of the image of our experience **fade away**. Finally, certain information is then transferred to long-term memory in a section in the frontal lobe of the brain known as the cerebral cortex. Scientists think this process may happen while we are sleeping, but exactly how the information is transferred from one area of the brain to another is a mystery.

Memory Loss

Although memory function is difficult to understand and analyze, memory loss is something that many people experience and worry about as they age. In the past, neuroscientists believed that age-related memory loss was associated with total numbers of brain cells. The theory was that the brain contained a **finite** number of neurons, and as we got older, we used up our stock of available cells. More recent research suggests that this may not be so and that neurogenesis, or the manufacture of new brain cells, may take place throughout a lifetime. Also, there is now evidence that damage to the hippocampus may play an important role in memory loss. Studies conducted on patients who have suffered damage to this area of the brain show that while they can still recall memories stored before the brain was damaged, they are unable to remember new facts. In addition, diseases associated with old age, such as Alzheimer's, and other problems involving short- and long-term memory loss, are now being traced to possible damage to the hippocampus.

Improving Memory

Research suggests that the power to retrieve information can be influenced by food and sleep. Vitamin E is, for example, able to break down chemicals, known as free radicals, that are thought to damage brain cells. Studies suggest that eating foods containing vitamin E, such as green vegetables,
40 is one way of reducing age-related memory loss. Though there is no **definitive** proof, there are others who believe that herbs such as ginseng and ginkgo help to improve both concentration and memory **retention**. Research on short-term memory indicates that getting a good night's sleep can also help one to **recollect** things more clearly.

Although the exact process by which memories are coded and retrieved remains a mystery, there is
45 no doubt that eating the right foods and getting **sufficient** amounts of sleep can help us make the best use of our brains' remarkable ability to store and recall information.

Reading Comprehension:
Check Your Understanding

A Decide whether the following statements about the reading are true (T) or false (F). If you check (✔) false, correct the statement to make it true.

	T	F
1 *Hippocampus* is taken from the Latin word for seahorse.		
2 The process of memory creation is fully understood.		
3 Even elderly people might be able to create new brain cells.		
4 Ginseng and ginkgo are proven to aid memory.		

B Complete the sentences with information from the reading. Write no more than three words for each answer.

1 Some people such as Gert Mittring have _____.
2 Images sent to the hippocampus are stored temporarily in _____.
3 In the past, scientists thought that age-related memory loss occurred as people lost _____.
4 Besides eating things, memory can be improved by getting enough _____.

C Critical Thinking

Discuss these questions with a partner.

1 Why do scientists still know so little for sure about the brain's memory processes?

2 What are some of your earliest memories? Do you think they have faded over time?

A For each group, circle the word that does not belong. The words in *italics* are vocabulary items from the reading.

Vocabulary Comprehension:
Odd Word Out

1 *definitive*	authoritative	clear-cut	innocuous
2 remarkable	*extraordinary*	extravagant	amazing
3 dismantle	take apart	*fade away*	separate
4 secure	limited	confined	*finite*
5 *recollect*	recall	remember	reap
6 keeping	*retention*	maintenance	discrimination
7 bring back	fulfill	*retrieve*	recapture
8 ultimate	highest	unmatchable	*sufficient*
9 *transform*	change	distinguish	alter

B Complete the sentences below using the vocabulary in *italics* from A. Be sure to use the correct form of the word.

1 With so many workers leaving the company, _____ of good employees has become a priority.

2 Many male breadwinners are being _____ into stay-at-home dads.

3 Because many players were confused, the _____ rules to the new video game were published and distributed by the company.

4 No, thank you, I don't need any more money. The amount I make is _____ for me.

5 The fireworks suddenly lit up the night sky, but their colors soon _____.

6 Complete the analogy: _____ is to *infinite* as *limited* is to *unlimited*.

7 Will you help me look for my car? I can't _____ where I parked it.

8 My brother has a(n) _____ memory. He can remember all the cards in a deck of 52.

9 Some dogs are trained to _____ birds after their owners have shot them.

Vocabulary Skill:

The Root Word
fic/fice

In this chapter you learned the word "sufficient," meaning "enough." This word is made by combining the root word "fic," meaning "to do" or "to make," with the prefix "suf-" and the suffix "-ent." "Fic," sometimes also written as "fice," is combined with other root words, prefixes, and suffixes to form many words in English. Verbs that end in "-fy" are related to the root "fic/fice."

A Match each root word or prefix with its meaning. Then check your answers with a partner.

1 bene-_____
2 de-_____
3 magna_____
4 pro-_____
5 sign_____
6 spec_____
7 sub-/suf-_____

a. to mark, to mean
b. great, large
c. under, beneath
d. good, well
e. forward
f. not, away, down
g. look

B For each word, study the different parts. Then, write the part of speech and a simple definition. Use your dictionary to help you. Share your ideas with a partner.

Word	Part of Speech	Definition
1 sufficient	noun	enough, adequate
2 beneficial		
3 deficit		
4 defy		
5 insignificant		
6 magnificent		
7 magnify		
8 proficient		
9 specify		
10 specification		

C Complete the sentences using some of the words from the chart. Be sure to use the correct form of the word.

1 I saw a _____ exhibit at the Museum of Modern Art yesterday—some of the finest painting and sculpture I've ever seen.
2 Danny is _____ in two languages in addition to English.
3 Does the class syllabus _____ which unit we should read first?
4 In order to see a human cell with your eyes, you'll need to _____ it using this machine.

Chapter 2: *Words to Remember*

A How good is your memory in each of these areas? Check the answer that is true for you.

Your memory for . . .	Poor	So-so	Good	Excellent
1 people's names				
2 how to get to places				
3 people's faces				
4 telephone numbers				
5 appointments				
6 song lyrics				
7 the taste of foods				
8 vocabulary				

B Discuss your answers from A with a partner.

Before You Read:
How Good Is Your Memory?

A Scan the reading passage to find the answers to these questions.

1 How many methods of memory enhancement are outlined in the passage?
2 What is the meaning of the word *mnemonics*?
3 What images might be used to represent the word *tremendous*?
4 To use the method of loci, what do you need to visualize?
5 When using the grouping method, what can you be creative about?

B Compare your answers with a partner.

C Read through the passage, then answer the questions that follow.

Reading Skill:
Scanning

> When we need to find certain information in a text, we move our eyes quickly across the page. When we see part of the text that might have our information, we read only that section. Scanning allows us to save time on tests, when searching for information on the Internet, etc.

Words to Remember

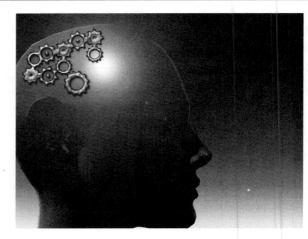

Expert opinions differ on the specific number of words a second-language learner needs to know to achieve fluency, but they generally agree that it is several thousand. Many language learners have
5 at some point wished that they could simply insert a computer chip into their memories containing all the vocabulary of the target language. Although that isn't yet **feasible**, with training, the potential of the human memory can be unlocked. One way that many teachers suggest accelerating the vocabulary-building process is by using *mnemonics*.
10 Simply put, mnemonics are methods used to help one remember information that is otherwise difficult to recall. There are a wide variety of methods, and different ones work better for different people. The method of loci is a visual method that involves associating words with **landmarks** along a familiar path. The grouping method **enhances** recall by organizing similar ideas together. Finally, in the method of **vivid** associations, target words are **linked** to very memorable images in
15 the mind for easier retrieval.

1 The method of loci

This method can be used to remember lists of words. Before using this method, it is necessary to **visualize** a path that you know well—the way to school or to work, for example. Next, looking at your list of words, you'll need to create a visual image for each word. For example,
20 for the word "accelerate," you might choose the image of a racecar; an image for the word "**tremendous**" might be a dinosaur. Creating these images may take a little practice. Then, visualize yourself progressing along the path you chose, **depositing** the images associated with the words at landmarks along the way—a racecar at the convenience store, a dinosaur in the park, etc. Finally, put away the list and move along the path in your mind again, recalling as
25 many words as you can.

2 The grouping method

Try to memorize the following group of words: *radio, pencil, index card, notebook, book, marker, magazine, newspaper, stereo, pen, MP3 player, paper*. You'll probably have more success if you divide the list into smaller groups: things you write with, things you write on, things you read,
30 and things you listen to. You'll probably find that you are able to recollect more words. When word lists you need to memorize for tests aren't so clearly divisible, you can be creative about making groups of words.

3 The method of vivid associations

To fix the memory of a new word in your mind, it can help to associate it with an image that
35 is vivid in some way—colorful, funny, embarrassing, beautiful, etc. For example, if you are trying

to remember the meaning of the word "tremendous," you might associate it with tremendously large *trees* and *men*. This vivid image is connected to the word not only in meaning, but also in the sound of the first two syllables of the word. This type of pairing of meaning, sound, and images can help you memorize new words more quickly.

40 What these three methods of enhancing memory have in common is the idea of *active learning*. While it is certainly possible to **absorb** a great deal of information by passively listening or reading, there is no guarantee that the information will enter your memory and be retained. We've looked at just a few of the many types of mnemonic devices that can be applied by language learners. Depending on your own learning style, one may work better than another for you. Try a variety of 45 methods and find the ones that work best for you.

A Choose the best answer for each question or statement about the reading. Try not to look back at the reading for the answers.

Reading Comprehension:
Check Your Understanding

1 What is the author's purpose in writing this passage?
   a. to introduce useful memory enhancing techniques
   b. to entertain the reader with extraordinary tricks of memory
   c. to demonstrate his or her superior memory skills

2 According to experts, how many words are necessary to achieve fluency in a second language?
   a. several hundred   **b.** several thousand   **c.** several million

3 According to the reading, what do the three memory methods have in common?
   a. grouping   **b.** use of a path   **c.** active learning

4 In the method of vivid associations, which of the following associations would be the best to use for the word *clockwork*?
   a. a clock on a wall
   b. a human-like clock working on other clocks
   c. your clock at work

B Decide whether the following statements about the reading are true (T) or false (F). If you check (✔) false, correct the statement to make it true.

	T	F
1 The potential of the human memory is quite limited.		
2 To use the method of loci, you need to mentally place images along a path.		
3 The grouping method advises us to break lists into smaller lists.		
4 A boring image is useful in the method of vivid associations.		
5 Not all mnemonic devices are suitable for all people.		

C Critical Thinking

Discuss these questions with a partner.

1 Do you wish that you could insert a computer chip into your head that would allow you to speak any language fluently? Why or why not?

2 Which of the three methods in the passage do you like the most? Explain your answer.

Vocabulary Comprehension:
Word Definitions

A **Look at the list of words and phrases from the reading. Match each with a definition on the right.**

1 deposit _____   a. an easily recognized place
2 enhance _____   b. to improve the quality of something
3 feasible _____   c. bright, colorful, or intense
4 absorb _____   d. to leave something somewhere, e.g., money in a bank
5 landmark _____   e. very great in amount or level
6 linked _____   f. able to be made, done, or achieved
7 tremendous _____   g. to form a picture in your mind
8 visualize _____   h. to take in; to learn and understand
9 vivid _____   i. connected

B **Complete the sentences below using the vocabulary from A. Be sure to use the correct form of the word.**

1 There is _____ pressure on many high school students to study hard in order to enter a good university.

2 Lisa brightened up her appearance by wearing _____ colors instead of gray and brown.

3 His many successes in school _____ John's self-esteem greatly.

4 Believe it or not, I can still _____ the faces of my elementary school teachers.

5 There was so much new vocabulary on that course, I could _____ only half of the new words.

6 For most of us, it's not _____ to remember a list of 100 words in a day.

7 The ship _____ its cargo of computers at the city port.

8 Which New York City _____ should I visit—the Statue of Liberty or the Empire State Building?

9 The two islands are _____ by a long bridge.

A Review the different strategies you can use for associating and recalling vocabulary. Which do you commonly use?

Word Association: Linking one word to related words
e.g.: school-related words: teacher, student, classroom, books

Synonyms and Antonyms
e.g.: definitive = certain; ≠ unsure

Word Families
e.g.: attend, attention, attentive

Word Pairings
e.g.: hot coffee (not burning coffee)

Idioms
e.g.: a last resort

Root Words, Prefixes, and Suffixes
e.g.: the root fic/fice; the prefix re-

Mnemonic Aids

a. Draw a picture that is related to the word or words.
b. Relate the sound or spelling of the new word to a sound or spelling in your own language.
c. Rhyme the new word with a similar word.
d. Relate the words to furniture in a room or places in a city.
e. Create a sentence or story using the words.
f. Combine all the words to make an acronym (e.g., HOMES for the Great Lakes: Huron, Ontario, Michigan, Erie, and Superior).

B Use one or more of the strategies above to help you recall the words below. Share your strategies with a partner.

> memory   retention   short cut   deficit   memorize   short recall
> retrieve   accelerating   mnemonic   forget   device
> memorization   panther   beneficial   long-term

Vocabulary Skill:
Vocabulary-Recall Strategies

In this chapter, you read about one method—mnemonics—that some people use for recalling new vocabulary. There are many different strategies that you can use to form associations between words in order to recall them more easily later. You've already practiced some of these strategies in different chapters of this book.

Real Life Skill:
Using Spelling Rules

In this unit, you've learned and reviewed some useful strategies for recalling vocabulary you learn in English. But what about spelling? In spite of the fact that one can use the "spell check" feature on the computer, it is still helpful to be familiar with some of the basic rules for spelling in English. There are also several mnemonic aids one can use to recall the rules.

A Review some common spelling rules in English. Say each of the words in the example column aloud.

Rule	Example	Tip
IE or EI	ceiling, neighbor, chief	I before E, except after C, or when sounded as A, as in *neighbor* and *weigh*.
Silent sounds	mnemonic, psychology, debt, through	Circle or highlight the silent letter. Rhyme the word with another word: *through-you*; *debt-jet* to remember pronunciation.
Dropping the final E	care - caring careful	Words ending in silent E: Drop the E if followed by a vowel (e.g., *caring*), but keep the E if followed by a consonant (*careful*).
Change Y to I	beauty - beautiful	Usually, in words that end with Y after a consonant, drop the Y and change it to I before adding a suffix.
Doubling letters	diner, dinner stop - stopped	Often (but not always!) long vowels take one consonant: short vowels, two.

B For each pair, (circle) the word that is spelled correctly. Check your answers with a partner.

1 foreign   forin
2 wieght   weight
3 though   thow
4 recieve   receive

5 timeing   timing
6 accommodate   accommodate
7 sunnyest   sunniest
8 runing   running

C Complete the spelling of the following words.

1 I was so embar_____ed when I tripped and fell. Everyone laughed at me.
2 Here's your r_____t for the coat you just bought. It was $150.
3 This person can predict the future: _____ic.
4 Can I use your k_____ to cut my meat?
5 Have you met my n_____e? She's my sister's daughter.

What Do You Think?

1 Being organized in different ways can make up for our limited human memories. How do you help yourself remember to do the things you have to do each day?
2 In what ways do you think human memory is different from computer memory? Are there any ways in which it is the same?

Discuss the following questions with a partner.

1 Can you name any of the superheroes in the comics above?
2 What superpowers does each of them possess?
3 Do you have a favorite fictional hero? Why do you like that hero?
4 In what forms of art and literature do these heroes appear?

Before You Read:
A Movie Review

A Think of a movie you saw recently. Complete this movie review chart.

Movie title	
Background information	
Setting	
Characters	
Plot	
Your opinion of the movie	

B Share the information you wrote in the chart with a partner.

Reading Skill:
Skimming for Opinions and Attitudes

Skimming can be useful when we want to get the general idea of all or part of a text. Positive or negative opinions and attitudes can be quickly understood by skimming while looking out for words and expressions that signal a positive or negative opinion or attitude. This can save time in discovering the author's point of view on a subject.

A Skim each of the paragraphs indicated and answer the questions about the author's opinions.

1 (Paragraph 1) When the author first heard about Allende's new book, he _____.
   a. wasn't optimistic   **b.** was thrilled   **c.** was overwhelmed
2 (Paragraph 1) The author's favorite actor in the role of Zorro is _____.
   a. Johnston McCully   **b.** Guy Williams   **c.** Walt Disney
3 (Paragraph 3) The author feels that Allende uses the outline of the story _____.
   a. to motivate the reader   **b.** in an interesting way   **c.** as in previous tales
4 (Paragraph 4) The author's reaction to the plot of the story is _____.
   a. positive   **b.** negative   **c.** undecided

B Check your answers with a partner.

C Read through the story, then answer the questions that follow.

Zorro: A Review

by Joshua Gibson

When I heard that Isabel Allende had written a new book called *Zorro,* my first thought was "Oh, no! Not another Zorro!" Though I respect Allende highly as a writer, I wondered what she could possibly do with the character that hadn't already

5 been done. Since the character of Zorro **debuted** in Johnston McCully's story "The Curse of Capistrano" nearly 90 years ago, Zorro has appeared in more than 60 stories and books, several movies, two TV series, cartoons and comic strips in various languages, and even a recent London play. Besides, I already

10 had my favorite Zorro—actor Guy Williams' version in the Disney TV series in the 1950s, which I had watched as a child. That Zorro was a little oversimplified, perhaps, but at least he was easy to understand and identify with. I wasn't so sure the character needed **updating**.

15 First, some background on the Zorro legend for those of you who may not remember. The setting is Spanish California in the early 1800s. Times are difficult, and the rulers use their power to exploit and **oppress** the common people. Zorro (Spanish for "fox") is the name for a masked man in a black cape who appears mysteriously whenever the people's rights are in danger. Zorro is

20 actually Diego de la Vega, the son of a Spanish officer and landowner. Diego **feels sorry for** the poor but cannot resist the rulers openly, so he uses a disguise. During the day, he plays a **self-effacing**, irresponsible scholar who prefers poetry to violent action. But, at night he changes into Zorro, the people's hero who seeks out and defeats the oppressors.

Allende works from this basic outline but does a couple of interesting things with it. First, she fills
25 in the details so we get a much better idea of the historical background. Second, she focuses on Diego's early life and explains what motivated him to become the defender of the poor. Since most of the previous tales take place after Zorro has appeared, this move back in time enables her to create largely her own story.

And what an amazing story it is! Allende takes us on an action-packed adventure from old California
30 to Spain with several stops in between. As it turns out, Diego is not only the son of a Spanish officer but also the grandson of the Native American wise woman White Owl, who instructs him in the ways of their people. In his childhood he has a dramatic encounter with a fox. The animal saves his life and becomes his guiding spirit. Later Diego is sent by his father to complete his education in Barcelona, Spain. Before he returns to California several years later, Diego has time to fall in love with a beautiful
35 young Spanish lady, hold off the **rival** for her hand, fight various evil-doers, travel across Spain with a group of gypsies, and be captured by a band of pirates near New Orleans. While telling this **extensive**

tale, Allende is able to show us how Diego becomes ever more **committed** to fighting **injustice** and learns to become an expert acrobat and swordsman. These are skills that Zorro will use to defeat his opponents.

40   Besides telling an exciting story Allende does a great job with her characters, who are much more complex and interesting than those in previous Zorro interpretations. For example, we find that Diego, who is a man of high principles when it comes to defending the oppressed, is also rather vain about his looks and cheats at cards when it serves his purpose. So in the end I have to say that I'm happy with Allende's updating of the Zorro legend. It's a version that appeals to adults and, after all, I'm not

45   a child anymore.

Reading Comprehension:
Check Your Understanding

A Decide whether the following statements about the reading are true (T) or false (F). If you check (✔) false, correct the statement to make it true.

	T	F
1 The author of this passage has enjoyed Zorro since childhood.		
2 Zorro's son is a Spanish officer and landowner.		
3 Previous Zorro stories also focused on his early life.		
4 Allende's Zorro tale takes place entirely in Spanish California.		
5 The characters in Allende's story are more complex than in previous Zorro stories.		

B Complete the sentences with information from the reading. Write no more than four words for each answer.

1   The first Zorro story was titled _____.
2   During the day, Zorro appears to be just _____.
3   Zorro's actual name is _____.
4   Although Zorro is a man of high principles, he sometimes _____.

C Critical Thinking

Discuss these questions with a partner.

1 Why do you think Isabel Allende chose to update the tale of Zorro?
2 Why do you think Zorro keeps his actual identity hidden?
3 Why does the author think Allende's version of *Zorro* will appeal to adults more than previous versions?

A

Vocabulary Comprehension:
Words in Context

The words in *italics* are vocabulary items from the reading. Read each question or statement and choose the correct answer. Compare your answers with a partner.

1 If an actress is *debuting* in a movie, she is probably _____.
   a. a veteran   **b.** not very experienced
2 Which of these is a form of *injustice*?
   a. discrimination   **b.** wisdom
3 Language is always *updating* itself, giving rise to _____ expressions.
   a. tried and true   **b.** ever new
4 I *feel sorry for* Makiko because ____.
   a. she just lost her job   **b.** I was rude to her yesterday
5 People say Paul is *self-effacing* because of his _____.
   a. usual modesty   **b.** vivid clothing
6 When two animals are *rivals*, they usually _____.
   a. live together   **b.** fight
7 When the doctor said Ken's injuries were *extensive*, I realized that _____.
   a. he might die   **b.** he was in no danger
8 If a husband and wife are *committed* to each other, their marriage _____.
   a. has a chance of lasting   **b.** is in trouble from the start
9 It is usually in places where people are very *oppressed* that _____.
   a. tourism increases   **b.** revolutions occur

B Answer the questions. Share your answers with a partner.

1 What is something that you are *committed* to doing this year?
2 Do you know when your favorite actor made his/her *debut* in a movie?
3 How do you keep *updated* with local news?
4 When was the last time you *felt sorry* for someone?
5 Would you describe any of your friends or family as *self-effacing*?
6 Have you ever been *rivals* with someone? What were you rivals for?
7 Do you know anyone who had suffered a form of *injustice*?
8 What is something that you have an *extensive* knowledge of?
9 Why might someone feel *oppressed*?

Vocabulary Skill:

Compound Adjectives

In this chapter, you learned the compound adjective "self-effacing." Compound adjectives are formed when two or more nouns, adjectives, adverbs, or the participle form of a verb (e.g., "dressed," "looking") are combined to modify a noun.

A **Look at how compound adjectives are formed.**

1 Some compound adjectives are formed by joining two words to form another word, e.g., an outspoken man, a secondhand car.

2 Other compound adjectives can be formed by combining two or more words using hyphens.
Is Yuri Gagarin well known in your country?   Is he a well-known astronaut?
Karina's daughter is five years old.   Karina has a five-year-old daughter.

3 Some compound adjectives are fixed—the word order is always the same, and they are always hyphenated.
He's a self-effacing guy.   These statistics are out-of-date.

B **What do you think the following compound adjectives mean? Complete the sentences with the correct adjective, then write a simple definition for each.**

> up-to-the-minute   over-the-counter   out-of-the-way
> matter-of-fact   middle-aged

1 In order to have some privacy, Erik and Laura stayed at a(n) _____ villa in the Colorado mountains.
Definition: _____

2 If you want _____ information on the election results, tune in to channel 4.
Definition: _____

3 I don't know exactly what the robber looked like; he had grayish hair and appeared to be _____.
Definition: _____

4 In the United States, you can't buy medicine such as antibiotics _____. You can only get them with a prescription.
Definition: _____

5 Antonio talked about failing his test in a very _____ way; it didn't seem to bother him at all.
Definition: _____

C **Now write three sentences using any of the compound adjectives you have learned. Share your ideas with a partner.**

1 _____
2 _____
3 _____

Chapter 2: From Comic Books to Graphic Novels

Discuss the following questions with a partner.

1 Which comic books did you read as a child?
2 How does reading comic books compare to reading novels?
3 What foreign comic books do you know?
4 Do you think comic books can cover serious topics?

A Read the statements below. Write **M** next to the statement that is the main idea of the paragraph. Write **S** next to the statement that is a supporting idea.

Paragraph 2

1 Comic book artists in several European countries, including France, Belgium, and Italy, also developed their own styles with original themes. _____
2 Comic books probably started in America, but they became popular around the world, and different comic book traditions developed in various countries. _____

Paragraph 3

3 You can still buy the magazine-like comic books, but by the 1970s a new form had appeared. _____
4 This was a longer, more expensive, hardbound publication often sold in regular bookstores. _____

Paragraph 4

5 Similarly, *Watchman* by Alan Moore and Dave Gibbons presents a series of complex, interesting stories in which the superheroes are more like regular human beings with all their faults and problems. _____
6 The appearance of a number of successful cartoon stories with mature content in the mid-1980s helped to establish the popularity of the new form. _____

B Compare your answers with a partner. Then scan the paragraphs to find the sentences and to find other supporting ideas.

C Now read through the passage and answer the questions that follow.

Reading Skill:
Identifying Main and Supporting Ideas

> Most paragraphs have a main idea, or topic, that tells us what that paragraph is about. Often, you will find the main idea talked about in the first or second sentence of a paragraph. Supporting ideas usually follow the main idea. Sentences containing supporting ideas explain or give us more information about the main idea.

From Comic Books to Graphic Novels

Originally they were called comic books, or comics **for short**. These were those picture or cartoon stories with **dialogue** that became very popular with young people in the United States in the 1940s and 1950s. Despite their name, they were not 5 always funny, and they were more like magazines than books because they were shorter, cheaper, and appeared **periodically** (often once a month) in newsstands at local stores. Many were about the adventures of superheroes such as Superman, Batman, and Wonder Woman. These were individuals with 10 special powers who fought against evil and injustice. The end of every story was never **in doubt**: the superhero, as the representative of the "good guys," always defeated the "bad guys," or the characters that represented the evil forces in the world.

Comic books probably started in America, but they became popular around the world, and different comic book traditions developed in various countries. In Japan, comic books are called 15 manga. Manga developed out of a combination of ukiyo-e (a drawing style dating back to the end of the 18th century) and Western techniques. Comic book artists in several European countries, including France, Belgium, and Italy, also developed their own styles with original themes. For example, in the 1930s the Franco-Belgian artist Hergé created the character Tintin, a reporter who travels to different countries to investigate stories. Many of the stories in the Tintin series were 20 based on real historical events such as Hitler's **conquest** of Austria in 1938. As a result, it was much more political and reality-based than the typical superhero-type comics found in the United States.

You can still buy the magazine-like comic books, but by the 1970s a new form had appeared. This was a longer, more expensive, hardbound **publication** often sold in regular bookstores. 25 The **content** clearly aimed at an older, more **mature** reader. Adventure stories with superheroes remained popular, but the new characters were deeper and more true-to-life, and the stories were more complex. To distinguish this new type of picture book from the earlier youth-oriented form, it was sometimes called a graphic novel.

The appearance of a number of successful cartoon stories with mature content in the mid-1980s 30 helped to establish the popularity of the new form. The transition from old to new style is perhaps clearest in Frank Miller's *Batman: The Dark Knight Returns*. In this story, an older Batman lives in a world where both the "good guys" and the "bad guys" have to make difficult moral choices.

Similarly, *Watchmen* by Alan Moore and Dave Gibbons presents a series of complex, interesting stories in which the superheroes are more like regular human beings with all their **faults** and problems. *Watchmen* became very popular and was the only graphic novel on *Time* magazine's list of the best 100 books since 1923. Finally, in *Maus*, by Art Spiegelman, we have an original graphic novel that totally breaks with the superhero theme. Maus tells us the story of mice, inspired by Spiegelman's Jewish parents, who struggled against the Nazis during World War II.

People have become more familiar with the new graphic novels, but many still find the term confusing. To some, graphic novels are just comic books, only longer. And the fact that the expression has become an important advertising tool hasn't helped. For example, some publishers have put together some of their old superhero series and are now selling them as "graphic novels." As a result, some of the new creators have decided not to use the term to describe their original works. Instead, they prefer expressions such as picture novella, graphic album, or original graphic novel.

A **Choose the best answer for each question or statement below. Try not to look back at the reading for the answers.**

Reading Comprehension:
Check Your Understanding

1 The topic of the reading passage is _____.
   a. a short history of a popular art form
   b. how graphic novels developed in the West
   c. why comics and graphic novels are worthwhile entertainment

2 According to the reading passage, where did comic books probably start?
   a. Japan   **b.** America   **c.** Belgium

3 What is the occupation of Hergé's character Tintin?
   a. a soldier   **b.** a doctor   **c.** a reporter

4 To distinguish them from comic books, the new hardbound, adult-oriented books were called _____.
   a. comic strips   **b.** graphic novels   **c.** manga

B **Decide whether the following statements about the reading are true (T) or false (F). If you check (✔) false, correct the statement to make it true.**

	T	F
1 In mature graphic novels, the battle between good and evil isn't so simple.		
2 *Maus* is the story of superheroes resisting the Nazis in World War II.		
3 Some people think graphic novels are just long comic books.		
4 Another term for "graphic novel" is "picture comic."		

C Critical Thinking

Discuss these questions with a partner.

1 Do you think graphic novels could or should be used in schools for the purposes of education?
2 What style of drawing in comic books or graphic novels do you prefer?

Vocabulary Comprehension:
Odd Word Out

A For each group, circle the word that does not belong. The words in *italics* are vocabulary items from the reading.

1	*conquest*	inhibition	takeover	invasion
2	stigma	*content*	ideas	subject matter
3	discussion	state	*dialogue*	talk
4	imperfection	shortcoming	dilemma	*fault*
5	*for short*	abbreviated	as a nickname	sue
6	deposit	*publication*	magazine	book
7	*in doubt*	uncertain	injustice	unsure
8	older	adult	juvenile	*mature*
9	*periodically*	competently	on occasion	from time to time

B Complete the sentences using the words in *italics* from A. Be sure to use the correct form of the word.

1 My sister is a well-known writer. Her stories have appeared in several

_____.

2 While seals spend most of their time in the sea, they _____ pull themselves out of the water onto dry land.

3 Marla's mother won't let her watch that TV show because of its violent

_____.

4 While young tigers are playful, _____ ones are dangerous and make poor pets.

5 The two characters in the play have a long _____ in the third scene.

6 Shlomo's biggest _____ is that he gets angry very quickly.

7 My name is Alexander, but you can call me Al _____.

8 After his successful _____ of France, Hitler turned his attack to England and to Russia.

9 Jennifer studied so hard for the exam, a high score was never

_____.

A Complete the chart below using the antonyms in the box.

Vocabulary Skill:
Antonyms

> An antonym is a word or phrase that has the opposite meaning of another word or phrase. One way of increasing your vocabulary is by learning antonyms.

| popular | can't stand | good point | evil |
| unrealistic | superior | juvenile | |

Vocabulary	Antonym
1 mature	
2 good	
3 tolerate	
4 unpopular	
5 true-to-life	
6 inferior	
7 fault	

B Complete the personal ad below using the antonyms from the chart in A. Check your answers with a partner.

Comic superheroes such as Batman, Superman, and Spiderman continue to be (1)_____ with millions of people. However, I (2)_____ them, because they have nothing to do with our everyday lives. I mean, they're completely (3)_____—normal people just don't have superpowers, and we don't spend our time fighting (4)_____ all day long. I prefer mature graphic novels, not (5)_____ comic books. Their plots are far (6)_____ to comic book plots, and another (7)_____ is that they are usually very original.

Real Life Skill:

Reading Online Movie Reviews

A great deal of information is available about movies on the Internet. There are reviews of every popular movie ever made, both new and old. The Internet again proves itself to be a useful tool when researching movie information.

A Think of two movies and find reviews for them online. Use the title of the movie plus "movie review" as keywords for your search.

B Scan the websites you found for information to complete the charts.

Movie title	
Review website	
Cast	
Director	
Movie rating	
Plot summary	
Good points/faults	

Movie title	
Review website	
Cast	
Director	
Movie rating	
Plot summary	
Good points/faults	

C Share the information you found with a partner.

What Do You Think?

1 If you could be any superhero in the world, which one would you choose to be and why?
2 Do you like Hollywood movies about superheroes? Why or why not?
3 What other forms of art, literature, or media are becoming popular with young people these days?

Fluency Strategy: *Thinking* ACTIVEly *While Reading*

In order to become a more fluent reader, remember to follow the six points of the **ACTIVE** approach—before, while, and after you read. See the inside front cover for more information on the **ACTIVE** approach.

Activate Prior Knowledge

Before you read, it's important to think about what you already know about the topic, and what you want to get out of the text.

A Look at the passage on the next page. Read only the title and look at the picture. What do you think the article is about? Why do you think Korean students at GBS High School might be unusual?

B Now read the first paragraph of the passage. What do you know about Asian and Pacific American students in the United States? Why do you think the percentage, particularly of Korean students, is so high in this school? Discuss with a partner.

Cultivate Vocabulary

As you read, you may come across unknown words. Remember, you don't need to understand all the words in a passage to understand the meaning of the passage. Skip the unknown words for now, or guess at their meaning and come back to them later. Note useful new vocabulary in your vocabulary notebook—see page 6 for more advice on vocabulary.

A Now read the first paragraph of the passage. Circle any words or phrases you don't know. Can you understand the rest of the paragraph even if you don't understand those items?

B Write the unknown words here. Without using a dictionary, try to guess their meaning. Use the words around the unknown word and any prefixes, suffixes, or word roots to help you.

New word/phrase   I think it means:

_____   _____

_____   _____

Think About Meaning

As you read, think about what you can infer, or "read between the lines," for example about the author's intention, attitudes, and purpose for writing.

Read the opening paragraph again and discuss these questions with a partner.
Who do you think this article was written by? Whom do you think it was written for? Who do you think reads *Asian Week* magazine? Why do you think the writer is interested in this topic? Why do you think the interactions of the Korean American students were the subject of an article?

Increase Reading Fluency

To increase your reading fluency, it's important to monitor your own reading habits as you read. Look again at the tips on page 8. As you read, follow these tips.

Now read the whole passage "Korean Americans at GBS High School." As you read, check your predictions from "Think About Meaning."

Korean Americans at GBS High School

Glenbrook South (GBS) High School is in a suburb of Chicago, Illinois, in the United States. It is an award-winning school with a highly competent teaching staff. It has over 400 Asian Pacific American students—over 17 percent of the students in the school. Of these, the majority are Korean American. This is very unusual in a state where Korean Americans are less than 1 percent of the population. The interactions of the Korean American students at GBS were the subject of an article in *Asian Week* magazine.

Different Korean American students react differently to being in a high school where most students are white. Professor Pyong Gap Min, an expert on Korean life in America, believes that Korean Americans in this situation can sometimes feel inhibited or ashamed of their Korean identity. *Asian Week* interviewed a number of GBS students, and each had a different attitude.

Eighteen-year-old Alice said that she used to spend time only with Korean American friends. Although she felt secure with those friends, she found herself motivated to form closer relationships with non-Koreans, too. She said that she felt she was missing out on new experiences and challenges.

Seventeen-year-old John moved in the opposite direction. In junior high school, most of John's friends were white. After coming to GBS, his sense of his Korean American identity was restored, and he decided to have mainly Korean American friends. He feels that he and his Korean American friends understand each other better. For example, they understand about severe parental pressures to succeed at school; John felt his white friends couldn't really understand.

Sixteen-year-old Paul has some Korean American friends, but he says he spends most of his time with his white friends. He is often the only Asian American in the group, but he doesn't mind. What Paul likes about the white culture is that he can be more radical—he can be as loud and funny as he wants to be. He says he doesn't see as much of that among the Asian students.

Without belittling the importance of what these students had to say, it's important to remember that their opinions at this phase of their lives are bound to change as they grow into adulthood. But these honest opinions can help us better understand issues of cultural relations, and their honesty might help Americans from different cultural groups to get along better in the future.

Verify Strategies

To build your reading fluency, it's important to be aware of how you use strategies to read, and to consider how successfully you are using them.

Use the questions in the Self Check on the next page to think about your use of reading strategies.

Evaluate Progress

Evaluating your progress means thinking about how much you understood from the passage, and how fluently you were able to read the passage to get the information you needed.

Check how well you understood the passage by answering the following questions.

1 What does the passage mainly discuss?
   a. how Korean American students interact among themselves and with others
   b. why Illinois is a very special state
   c. how an Illinois high school welcomes Korean American students
   d. different opinions of the friends of Korean American students

2 According to the first paragraph, what makes GBS an unusual high school?
   a. It is in the state of Illinois, which is very far from Korea.
   b. All its Korean American students prefer to have white friends.
   c. It is in the suburbs where the Korean American population is low.
   d. It has a high percentage of Korean American students compared to the percentage in the state.

3 According to paragraph 2, who can sometimes feel inhibited or ashamed?
   a. students who react differently to being Korean American
   b. Korean American students when they are interviewed
   c. Korean American students in a mostly white school
   d. GBS students who have different attitudes

4 Who interviewed the three Korean American students?
   a. *Asian Week*
   b. Professor Pyong Gap Min
   c. the GBS teaching staff
   d. other GBS students

5 Which statement best summarizes Alice's attitude?
   a. She feels that her white friends don't really understand her.
   b. She likes her Korean American friends but wants to have non-Korean friends, too.
   c. She feels she is missing out on experiences with her Korean American friends.
   d. She doesn't feel secure in her relationships with non-Koreans.

6 Which phrase could best be substituted for "radical" in line 28?
   a. angry and dangerous
   b. very expressive
   c. polite and considerate
   d. selfish and greedy

7 What DOESN'T the author think about the opinions of the three students?
   a. They could change.
   b. They are unimportant.
   c. They are honest.
   d. They could help people in the future.

Self Check

A Here is a list of all the reading skills in Active Skills for Reading Book 3. For each skill, say whether you found the skill useful, not useful, or if you need more work with it. Check (✔) the appropriate box.

Reading skill	Useful	Not useful	Needs work
Arguing For and Against a Topic			
Identifying Cause and Effect			
Identifying Fact Versus Theory			
Identifying Main and Supporting Ideas			
Identifying Main Ideas within Paragraphs			
Identifying Meaning from Context			
Making Inferences			
Predicting			
Previewing			
Recognizing Facts			
Recognizing Sequence Markers			
Scanning			
Skimming for Opinions and Attitudes			
Skimming for the Main Idea			

B Here are the four fluency strategies covered in the Review Units. For each strategy, say whether you found it useful, not useful, or if you need more work with it. Check (✔) the appropriate box.

Fluency strategy	Useful	Not useful	Needs work
Reading with a purpose: DRTA			
KWL			
SQ3R			
Reading ACTIVEly			

C Look again at the *Are You an Active Reader?* quiz on page 10 and complete your answers again. How has your reading fluency improved since you started this course

Fluency Practice

Time yourself as you read through the passage. Try to read as fluently as you can. Record your time in the Reading Rate Chart on page 208. Then answer the questions on the following page.

http://www.asrinfo.net/memorychamps

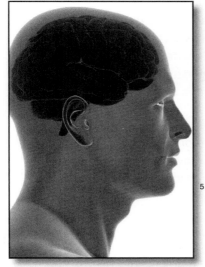

You Can Be a World Memory Champion!

Every year, people with extraordinary memory skills compete at that definitive memory event: the World Memory Championships. The tasks they are required to do require tremendous powers of

5   memory retention: looking at and reciting a two-page poem; recollecting a page of 40-digit numbers; remembering the order of 52 cards in a deck; memorizing the names of 110 people after looking at their pictures; and several other demanding tasks.

10 Completing any of these tasks may not seem feasible for the average person, but scientific evidence seems to show that even someone with average skills can, through training, enhance his or her memory skills and be transformed into a memory champion.

One memory champion explained his method of recalling the order of the cards in a deck. Previously, he linked a person, an action, and a thing to each card in the deck. For

15 example, the king of hearts is Elvis Presley, eating quickly, a peanut butter sandwich. The three of spades is Rocky Balboa, boxing, Madison Square Garden. The ten of hearts is William Shakespeare, writing *Hamlet*, a broken pen. Then any group of three cards creates a vivid image that won't quickly fade away. For example: king-ten-three becomes Elvis Presley writing *Hamlet* in Madison Square Garden—a memorable image.

20 Still, even having created images for each group of three cards, it is difficult to keep them in order. This is done using the *method of loci*. First, visualize a path that is well known to you. Along the path there need to be landmarks that you know well. Into each landmark, you mentally deposit one of the vivid images you created. Then, in your mind, go back and

follow the path, stopping at each landmark along the way. With practice, you'll be able to remember a deck of cards in order.

But, what about people with naturally superior memories? We've all heard of people with photographic memories—the ability to memorize anything just by looking at it. Rajan Mahadevan, born in India in 1957, seemed to have such a memory. By the age of five, he was able to remember the license plate numbers of a parking lot full of cars. He was also able to remember a string of 31,811 digits. One book claimed that his memory power was a natural talent. Later, however, Mahadevan visited with K. Anders Ericsson, a psychologist who believes that memory is a matter of sufficient training, not talent. They discussed Mahadevan's memory achievements, and Mahadevan explained that he had spent 1,000 hours and used memory techniques to memorize the 31,811 digits. He admitted that it was hard training that allowed him to do it, not a special memory.

The 2006 World Memory Championships were held at Oxford University in England. The winner, Clemens Mayer from Germany, is the perfect example of how someone with an average memory can enhance it. Just three years before, Mayer had seen another memory champion on television, memorizing the order of cards in a deck. Mayer was a champion runner, without any special memory skills. Still, he thought he could do it, and he began to work hard at training his memory. He spent two hours a day practicing, and succeeded. At the 2006 championships, he memorized the cards in about one minute.

Although many still think that people have either good or bad memories from birth, that need not be true. Don't be satisfied with finite memory power. By using the methods of grouping, linking to vivid images, and the method of loci, we can all enhance our memories. You might even become the next World Memory Champion!

608 words   Time taken _____

Reading Comprehension

1 The author's purpose in writing is to _____.
   a. praise World Memory Champions
   b. explain how only special people have great memories
   c. give the history of the World Memory Championships
   d. explain how a good memory is more a matter of training than of talent

2 Which memory task is not mentioned in the passage?
   a. remembering the order of a deck of cards
   b. memorizing a poem
   c. remembering a drawing
   d. memorizing names

3 Which of the following best expresses the essential information in paragraph 2?
   a. Each card has a person, action, and thing linked to it. These are used to form a memorable image for any group of three cards.
   b. Each card has an image linked to it. For groups of three cards, these images fade away, leaving one memorable image.
   c. A person, an action, and a thing are selected for each group of three cards, making sure the image is memorable.
   d. Each card has an image on it. These easy-to-remember images are then grouped in threes.

4 Why is the method of loci useful for memorizing the order of a deck of cards?
   a. It makes images even more vivid.
   b. It assists with remembering the order of the three-card groups.
   c. It allows landmarks to be more easily recalled.
   d. It lets you go back again if you forget.

5 According to the passage, what did a book claim to be true about Rajan Mahadevan?
   a. that his memory skill was a natural talent
   b. that he was good at remembering things since childhood
   c. that he had spent 1,000 hours learning memory techniques
   d. that his powers of memory were actually a hoax

6 According to the passage, what is true about Clemens Mayer?
   a. He was born with excellent memory skills.
   b. He learned memory skills from watching television.
   c. Three years before he won the championship, his memory was untrained.
   d. His running skills helped his memory training.

7 What tone does the author take in the final paragraph?
   a. negative
   b. encouraging
   c. neutral
   d. humorous

Review Reading 8: *Manga*, *Manhwa*, and *Manhua*

Fluency Practice

Time yourself as you read through the passage. Try to read as fluently as you can. Record your time in the Reading Rate Chart on page 208. Then answer the questions on the following page.

Manga, Manhwa, and Manhua

The combination of pictures with words to tell a story existed thousands of years ago in the ancient civilizations of Egypt and China. In more recent times, the
5 first published comic book using speech balloons to show dialogue is usually reported to be *The Yellow Kid*, which debuted in 1896. The content of early comic books was nearly always humorous—
10 E. Segar's famous *Popeye* is one example. In the early 20th century, however, comic book plots became more extensive, with many hero and adventure stories. Many Western comic books made their way to the
15 Far East, where they inspired new trends that continue to this day.

In the West, perhaps the best known type of East Asian comic book is the Japanese *manga*. In the 1950s and '60s, the Japanese artist Osamu Tezuka produced a variety of *manga* for children, such as *Kimba the White Lion* and *Astro Boy*. His books often
20 included mature, tragic themes. By the 1980s and '90s, *manga* was no longer just for young children. It had conquered the teenage and young adult markets as well. In fact, by the late 20th century, *manga* represented 40 percent of all Japanese publishing.

The form of comic book or graphic novel produced in South Korea is the *manhwa*. Much of early 20th century *manhwa* was used to speak out against oppression and injustice.
25 Around the time of the Korean War, *manhwa* also provided a welcome escape for young people. Today, South Korea is one of the most Internet-connected countries in the world, and many people prefer to read *manhwa* (or translations of rival *manga*) online

via computer or cell phone. In recent years, television dramas and movies have been based on *manhwa*. In general, interest in things Korean has been on the rise in the world recently, and interest in *manhwa* has increased.

There is a long tradition of comic books in Chinese. The arrival of printing techniques from the West in the 19th century allowed the growth of *lianhuantu*, a picture book intended to tell stories. The modern term for comic books and graphic novels written in Chinese is *manhua*. Most *manhua* are published in Hong Kong and in Taiwan. As in Korea, *manhua* comics have been used both for the expression of political opinions and as entertainment. Recently, a type of *manhua* called *wuxia* comics has become popular. These softcover or hardcover graphic novels usually involve martial arts combat. The famous story *Crouching Tiger, Hidden Dragon* can be read as a *wuxia* comic. A well drawn and well written *wuxia* comic can provide a similar experience to an exciting martial arts movie.

Asian comics have an influence in the West, where the market for them is growing quickly. Many top North American artists have been influenced by Asian comics. About 40 newspapers in North America have added Asian-style comic strips. The biggest consumer of *manga* outside of Japan is France. Ten million *manga* books are sold in France annually. There, traditional cartoons are being updated with a new style that combines Asian and European techniques. French and Japanese artists are working together on popular cartoons that have a more mature look.

Manga, *manhwa*, and *manhua* have all made great progress in recent decades. Their powerful influence has had an effect in the West, an influence which continues to strengthen. A growing base of committed fans outside Asia follows each new development with great interest. Internet technologies now allow fans to enjoy cartoons in new, more convenient ways, and Asian comics promise to be a lasting trend with influence across all forms of media.

600 words   Time taken _____

Reading Comprehension

1 What does the passage mainly discuss?
 a. competition among East Asian comics
 b. the future of East Asian comics in Europe
 c. the influence of Western comics on East Asian comics
 d. East Asian comic books and their relationship with the West

2 According to the first paragraph, which statement is true about early 20th century comic books?
 a. They had more extensive plots than earlier ones.
 b. They were the first comic books.
 c. They were nearly always humorous.
 d. They didn't have speech balloons.

3 Which of the following is an example of Japanese *manga*?
 a. *The Yellow Kid*
 b. *Popeye*
 c. *Astro Boy*
 d. *Manhwa*

4 According to paragraph 3, which statement about *manhwa* is not true?
 a. Many of them are translations of *manga*.
 b. They can be read on the Internet.
 c. Television dramas have been based on them.
 d. They have been used to speak out against injustice.

5 Which of the following is a Chinese martial arts comic?
 a. *lianhuantu*
 b. *manhua*
 c. *wuxia*
 d. *manhwa*

6 According to the passage, in which of these places are the most *manga* sold?
 a. Korea
 b. France
 c. the United States
 d. Hong Kong

7 In the final paragraph, what is the author's tone regarding the future of *manga*?
 a. humorous
 b. unfavorable
 c. critical
 d. optimistic

Vocabulary Index

Unit 1
Chapter 1

accessible /əkˈsesəbl/ *adj.* able to be entered or reached: *The opera house is accessible by bus, subway, or car.*

allure /əˈlʊər/ *n.* the attraction of something desirable or tempting: *Making a lot of money easily holds great allure for many people.*

colony /ˈkɒləni/ *n.* a region, country, or land of colonization, especially one controlled by a foreign power: *the (former) French colonies of North Africa*

facility /fəˈsɪləti/ *n.* service, including the physical area, provided by an organization: *The sports facility at that club includes tennis courts, a golf course, and a swimming pool.*

humid /ˈhjuːmɪd/ *adj.* having damp air (and uncomfortable weather): *Oh, it's so humid today; it's hard to breathe!*

intensify /ɪnˈtensɪfaɪ/ *v.* to get stronger, to make something stronger, to increase: *The noise from the party intensified as the clock struck midnight.*

off-season /ɔːf ˈsiːzn/ *adj., n.* not during the height of the tourist season: *We took a less costly, off-season cruise in the Caribbean during the off-season.*

procession /prəˈseʃn/ *n.* a parade: *A procession of marchers and bands moved down Main Street.*

wildlife sanctuary /ˈwaɪldlaɪf ˈsæŋktʃueri/ *n.* a safe, protected place for animals to live in their natural setting: *We saw many interesting animals as we walked through the wildlife sanctuary.*

Chapter 2

adapt /əˈdæpt/ *v.* to change, to function in a new way, to adjust: *She adapted (herself) quickly to her new job.*

affection /əˈfekʃn/ *n.* tender actions, such as hugging and kissing, caressing: *The child needs his mother's affection.*

conservative /kənˈsɜːrvətɪv/ *adj.* not showy, restrained in manner and dress: *Tomiko is a banker who wears a conservative business suit to work.*

critical /ˈkrɪtɪkl/ *adj.* pointing out faults, derogatory, disparaging: *The teacher wrote critical remarks on my paper about mistakes that I made.*

far-off /fɑːr ɔːf/ *adj.* distant, faraway: *He dreams of visiting far-off lands.*

gratitude /ˈgrætɪtuːd/ *n.* thankfulness, appreciation: *She showed her gratitude by saying, "Thank you!"*

locale /loʊˈkæl/ *n.* a place, a location for something that happens: *The movie director chose a new locale to shoot the final scenes of the film.*

sacred /ˈseɪkrɪd/ *adj.* holy: *For religious people, a wedding ceremony is sacred.*

tolerant /ˈtɒlərənt/ *adj.* accepting of different beliefs and behavior: *The boy's parents are tolerant of his naughty behavior.*

Unit 2
Chapter 1

cue /kjuː/ *n.* a signal to begin a particular action: *I didn't know where to go so I took my cue from the people leaving the elevator.*

decade /ˈdekeɪd/ *n.* a period of ten years: *the decade of the 1990s*

dictate /ˈdɪkteɪt/ *v.* to command, to say what someone must do: *The winner of a war can dictate to the loser the terms for peace.*

essential /ɪˈsenʃl/ *adj.* central, major: *The essential point is we must do what the contract says.*

idolize /ˈaɪdəlaɪz/ *v.* to admire greatly, to look up to: *Jane idolizes her older sister.*

imitate /ˈɪmɪteɪt/ *v.* to act the same way as another: *The boy imitates his father's way of talking.*

make a statement /meɪk ə ˈsteɪtmənt/ *phr. v.* to make one's opinion about something known publicly with words or actions: *They protested in front of town hall to make a statement about the war.*

synthetic /sɪnˈθetɪk/ *adj.* artificial, man-made: *Synthetic drugs are increasingly important for public health.*

trendy /ˈtrendi/ *adj.* fashionable, stylish: *Her clothes are very trendy.*

Chapter 2

crucial /ˈkruːʃl/ *adj.* extremely important, critical, decisive: *It is of crucial importance that we sign* *that contract for our future success.*

custom /ˈkʌstəm/ *n.* a habitual way of behaving that is special to a person, people, region, or nation: *It is a British custom to drink tea at four o'clock in the afternoon.*

cutting-edge /ˈkʌtɪŋ edʒ/ *adj.* most modern: *The designs of this company are cutting-edge.*

distinctive /dɪˈstɪŋktɪv/ *adj.* different from others, special: *Spices give that dish its distinctive flavor.*

exclusive /ɪkˈskluːsɪv/ *adj.* limited to people with a lot of money and high social position, restricted, prestigious: *an exclusive club, an exclusive neighborhood*

interior /ɪnˈtɪriə/ *adj.* of or about the inside of something: *The interior walls are painted white.*

reputation /ˌrepjuˈteɪʃn/ *n.* public opinion about the quality of something, such as a person's character: *She guards her reputation by being honest with everyone.*

revolution /ˌrevəˈluːʃn/ *n.* a big change, sometimes caused by force or war, especially in a government, economy, or field of study: *The Industrial Revolution changed how people worked and lived.*

ultimate /ˈʌltɪmət/ *adj.* last, highest: *The ultimate responsibility for this project belongs to the boss.*

Unit 3
Chapter 1

appalling /əˈpɔːlɪŋ/ *adj.* shocking, deeply offending: *The number of overweight school children today is appalling.*

awareness /əˈwernəs/ *n.* the state of being knowledgeable about something, an understanding: *How can we raise awareness about global warming?*

demand /dɪˈmænd/ *n.* the state of being much wanted: *There is a strong demand for this product in the market.*

die out /daɪ aʊt/ *phr. v.* to pass out of existence: *Dinosaurs died out millions of years ago.*

exploitation /ˌeksplɔɪˈteɪʃn/ *n.* a situation in which someone is being treated unfairly or being taken advantage of: *The exploitation of animals must come to an end immediately.*

extinct /ɪkˈstɪŋkt/ *adj.* no longer in existence, especially

a kind of plant or animal: *The passenger pigeon is an extinct species.*

factor /ˈfæktər/ *n.* a fact to be considered: *The high cost of labor is an important factor in the price of steel.*

intentionally /ɪnˈtenʃənli/ *adv.* with purpose, deliberately: *He lied intentionally to get ahead of the competition.*

vulnerable /ˈvʌlnərəbl/ *adj.* exposed, unprotected: *The soldiers were in a position vulnerable to attack by the enemy.*

Chapter 2

conduct /kənˈdʌkt/ *v.* to do something: *That store conducts business from 9:00 a.m. to 7:00 p.m.*

encounter /ɪnˈkaʊntə/ *n.* a meeting, usually unplanned: *She had an encounter with a drunk on the subway.*

era /ˈɪrə/ *n.* a time period with a general character: *The Eisenhower era in the United States was one of peace and prosperity.*

ethical /ˈeθɪkl/ *adj.* related to moral or correct behavior: *He found a woman's purse and did the ethical thing; he returned it to her.*

fertilize /ˈfɜːrtlaɪz/ *v.* to start the development of new life: *Male fish fertilize the eggs of female fish.*

fitting /ˈfɪtɪŋ/ *adj.* suitable, proper: *It was a fitting end to the story.*

frail /freɪl/ *adj.* physically weak: *His mother has grown old and frail.*

revive /rɪˈvaɪv/ *v.* to reawaken, to return someone to consciousness: *The paramedic revived a man who had lost consciousness.*

wander /ˈwɑːndə/ *v.* to go from place to place without a fixed plan or goal, to roam: *The travelers wandered from country to country.*

Unit 4
Chapter 1

calculation /ˌkælkjuˈleɪʃn/ *n.* an act of doing math: *Scientists use computers to help them make their calculations.*

cost of living /kɔːst əv ˈlɪvɪŋ/ *phr. n.* the cost of the necessities of life, such as food, housing, clothes, transportation, etc.: *The cost of living in cities like New York, Paris, and Tokyo is very high.*

dense /dens/ *adj.* crowded together: *a dense forest, dense traffic*

inflation /ɪnˈfleɪʃn/ *n.* a rise in prices and lowering of currency's value: *Inflation was so great that bread cost twice as much in June as it did in May.*

life expectancy /laɪf ɪkˈspektənsi/ *n.* the average age to which people can expect to live: *In the United States, the life expectancy of women is longer than that of men.*

property /ˈprɑːpərti/ *n.* land and buildings, real estate: *She owns property in California.*

realize /ˈriːəlaɪz/ *v.* to understand, to start to believe something is true: *He realizes now that he needs to go back to college for more education.*

soar /sɔːr/ *v.* to reach a higher level than usual: *The beautiful music soared.*

supply /səˈplaɪ/ *n.* a quantity of goods: *We need a supply of pens because we are out of them.*

_____ _____

Chapter 2

affluent /ˈæfluənt/ *adj.* wealthy, prosperous: *He is an affluent man.*

extravagant /ɪkˈstrævəgənt/ *adj.* too generous or expensive: *She gives extravagant gifts to her family for their birthdays.*

fortune /ˈfɔːrtʃuːn/ *n.* wealth, riches: *He made a fortune in the oil business.*

irate /aɪˈreɪt/ *adj.* very angry, infuriated, incensed: *The governor received irate letters and phone calls from people who didn't want higher taxes.*

keep up with /ˈkiːp ʌp wɪð/ *phr. v.* to stay level with: *She has two jobs to keep up with her rising bills.*

sensibly /ˈsensəbli/ *adv.* wisely: *She spends her hard-earned money sensibly.*

strike it rich /straɪk ɪt rɪtʃ/ *phr. v.* to make a lot of money: *After all his hard work, he finally struck it rich in the pet care business.*

unforeseen /ˌʌnfɔːrˈsiːn/ *adj.* unexpected, happening by accident: *Due to unforeseen circumstances (because of catching the flu), he could not go to the office.*

windfall /ˈwɪndfɔːl/ *n.* sudden good luck, especially unexpected money: *I had just bought the stock when I received a windfall of an extra dividend.*

_____ _____

Unit 5
Chapter 1

bloom /bluːm/ *v.* to flower: *Our apple tree bloomed last week.*

engrave /ɪnˈgreɪv/ *v.* to cut or carve words, pictures, or designs in metal, stone, etc.: *She engraved a winter scene on a copper plate for printing.*

eternal /ɪˈtɜːrnl/ *adj.* lasting forever, timeless: *People of many religions believe that God is eternal.*

fabric /ˈfæbrɪk/ *n.* cloth, material: *The sofa is covered with a soft cotton fabric.*

modesty /ˈmɒdəsti/ *n.* acting, behaving, or dressing in a way so as to not attract attention: *In some countries, women wear long skirts and long-sleeved tops as a sign of modesty.*

progress /ˈprɑːgrəs/ *v.* to move ahead: *He is progressing nicely in his study of French.*

purity /ˈpjʊərəti/ *n.* the state of being clean, not dirty or polluted: *The color white is often used to symbolize purity.*

show off /ˈʃoʊ ɔːf/ *v.* to act in a way that calls attention to oneself: *The boy shows off by telling people his father is very rich.*

union /ˈjuːniən/ *n.* a joining of forces: *A union of nations brings peace to the world.*

_____ _____

Chapter 2

adopt /əˈdɑːpt/ *v.* to copy, to accept or start to use something new: *The boy adopts the same way of talking that his father has.*

appreciation /əˌpriːʃiˈeɪʃn/ *n.* gratitude, thankfulness: *The man showed his appreciation to the waiter by leaving him a big tip.*

associate /əˈsoʊʃieɪt/ *v.* to connect in the mind, to correlate: *I associate his bad behavior with his difficult childhood.*

corporation /ˌkɔːrpəˈreɪʃn/ *n.* a business with a legal status (incorporated) where the assets and debts belong to shareholders who are not responsible for them beyond the value of their stock: *When a corporation becomes bankrupt, its stock is of no value anymore.*

institution /ˌɪnstɪˈtuːʃn/ *n.* someone or something that is a necessary, longtime part of something: *Big Sunday dinners are an institution at Mom's house.*

interpretation /ɪnˌtɜːrprɪˈteɪʃn/ *n.* an explanation, a decision about what something means: *My interpretation of the Bible is different from my priest's.*

media /ˈmiːdiə/ *n.* used with a singular or plural verb, used with "the" to mean the combination of television, radio, news magazines, and large circulation newspapers: *The media report on every little thing that the President does.*

parliamentary /ˌpɑːrləˈmentri/ *adj.* belonging to the parliament: *All parliamentary announcements are usually reported first on television.*

version /ˈvɜːrʒn/ *n.* an account of something: *He told his own version of the funny story.*

Unit 6
Chapter 1

baffle /ˈbæfl/ *v.* not to understand something at all, to confuse completely: *His disappearance baffled the police.*

enigma /ɪˈnɪgmə/ *n.* a mystery, a puzzle: *No one knows what happened to the airplane; its disappearance is an enigma.*

insignificant /ˌɪnsɪgˈnɪfɪkənt/ *adj.* not important, without meaning: *We thought the book had too many insignificant details about George Washington's life and not enough history.*

intriguing /ɪnˈtriːgɪŋ/ *adj.* interesting, causing curiosity, fascinating: *Psychologists find human emotions intriguing.*

isolated /ˈaɪsəleɪtɪd/ *adj.* separated from others, alone: *It is hard to know what goes on in the isolated parts of the country.*

phenomenon /fəˈnɑːmɪnən/ *n.* a fact, event, or image that strikes one's attention and attracts interest: *Snow was a phenomenon he had never seen before.*

resemble /rɪˈzembl/ *v.* to look like someone or something else: *The boy resembles his father; they both have blond hair and blue eyes.*

speculate /ˈspekjuleɪt/ *v.* to guess about: *She is so quiet; we can only speculate about what she is thinking.*

witness /ˈwɪtnəs/ *v.* to see, to observe an incident: *He witnessed the auto accident and wrote a report.*

Chapter 2

burst into flames /bɜːrst ˈɪntə fleɪmz/ *phr. v.* to combust, to catch fire: *The stack of papers burst into flames within seconds.*

external /ɪkˈstɜːrnl/ *adj.* coming from the outside: *Children's experiences in school are affected by many external influences.*

function /ˈfʌŋkʃn/ *n.* purpose, use: *The computer has a number of important functions.*

inside-out /ˌɪnˈsaɪd aʊt/ *adj.* reversed: *Why are you wearing your jacket inside-out?*

put out /pʊt aʊt/ *v.* to extinguish a fire: *Firefighters put out the fire with a water hose.*

spontaneous /spɑːnˈteɪniəs/ *adj.* happening without being caused by something outside: *a spontaneous fire*

supposedly /səˈpoʊzɪdli/ *adv.* as it seems, so it is assumed: *They will supposedly arrive in time for dinner.*

ventilated /ˈventɪleɪtɪd/ *adj.* exposed to air, especially to a current of fresh air: *That room is well ventilated because of all the windows.*

victim /ˈvɪktɪm/ *n.* someone or something that suffers from an accident, crime, illness, or bad luck: *The accident victim was helped by ambulance attendants.*

Unit 7
Chapter 1

alternate /ɔːlˈtɜːrneɪt/ *v.* to move or switch back and forth: *We alternate between living in Florida in the winter and Maine in the summer.*

carbohydrate /ˌkɑːrboʊˈhaɪdreɪt/ *n.* any of a group of nutrients, such as sugar and starch, that provide the body with energy: *Grains and fruits are high in carbohydrates.*

do the trick /duː ðə trɪk/ *phr. v.* to work, to be effective: *Just rub a little salt on the stain and that will do the trick.*

fad /fæd/ *n.* a fashion that lasts a short time: *The current fad among young people is to wear baseball caps.*

fed up with /fed ʌp wɪð/ *phr. adj.* annoyed or angry about a bad situation that has existed for a long time, frustrated, disgusted: *I am completely fed* up with all of the false promises and delays.

fiber /ˈfaɪbər/ *n.* the part of a plant taken in as food that cannot be absorbed by the body: *Doctors say you should eat food that is high in fiber.*

moderate /ˈmɒdərət/ *adj.* in the middle, not large or small, modest: *He makes a moderate income.*

portion /ˈpɔːrʃn/ *n.* a small piece or section of a larger thing: *I put a portion of my salary in a savings account each month.*

veteran /ˈvetərən/ *adj.* having a lot of experience in a job, profession, or art: *He is a veteran newspaper reporter.*

Chapter 2

draw out /drɔː aʊt/ *v.* to extract: *The miners drew out oil from the ground.*

frantically /ˈfræntɪkli/ *adv.* in a very rushed manner, frenziedly: *Rescuers were frantically trying to save the drowning man.*

grateful /ˈɡreɪtfl/ *adj.* thankful: *I am grateful for the help that you have given to me.*

initial /ɪˈnɪʃl/ *adj.* beginning, first: *My initial good opinion of him changed with time.*

innocuous /ɪˈnɑːkjuəs/ *adj.* harmless: *The teacher's innocuous words don't make me angry, but they also don't teach me much.*

reckless /ˈrekləs/ *adj.* doing something dangerous without thinking, foolish, rash: *He is reckless when he drives his car too fast.*

supervisor /ˈsuːpərvaɪzər/ *n.* a person who supervises others and their work: *a supervisor of a manufacturing operation*

tumor /ˈtuːmər/ *n.* a growth of diseased tissue: *A surgeon removed a benign tumor from the patient's stomach.*

undertake /ˌʌndərˈteɪk/ *v.* to accept and begin work on something usually large and serious: *The government will undertake the building of a large courthouse.*

Unit 8
Chapter 1

ailment /ˈeɪlmənt/ *n.* an illness, especially a lasting condition: *His ailments include a mild heart condition and arthritis.*

deprived /dɪˈpraɪvd/ *adj.* prevented from having basic rights or necessities: *He is away from home and feels deprived of his loved ones.*

disorder /dɪsˈɔːrdər/ *n.* a sickness or disturbance (of the mind or body): *a stomach disorder*

distinguish /dɪˈstɪŋwɪʃ/ *v.* to see or understand differences, to discriminate: *That child cannot distinguish between right and wrong!*

distribution /ˌdɪstrɪˈbjuːʃn/ *n.* giving or dealing out (of something): *The Red Cross was responsible for the distribution of medical supplies.*

duration /duˈreɪʃn/ *n.* the time that something continues or exists: *We hope that the business recession (illness, rainy season, etc.) will be of short duration.*

exposure /ɪkˈspoʊʒər/ *n.* the state of being unprotected: *The lost mountain climbers suffered from exposure.*

physiological /ˌfɪziəˈlɒdʒɪkl/ *adj.* pertaining to living bodies (humans, animals, and plants): *Stress creates emotional and physiological problems for people and animals.*

portrayal /pɔːrˈtreɪəl/ *n.* the act of portraying: *The actress's portrayal of the heroine in the film was outstanding.*

Chapter 2

analogy /əˈnælədʒi/ *n.* a situation or story similar to another that helps one to understand: *An analogy works like this: As a reservoir stores water, the mind stores knowledge.*

cargo /ˈkɑːrɡoʊ/ *n.* goods (usually in large amounts), freight: *Cargo is carried on ships, airplanes, and trucks.*

concept /ˈkɑːnsept/ *n.* a general idea that usually includes other related ideas: *Democracy is a concept that includes, among other things, the ideas of individual freedom and the right to vote.*

dismantle /dɪsˈmæntl/ *v.* to take apart, to break down into pieces: *A mechanic dismantled the engine to replace one part.*

far-fetched /ˈfɑːrˈfetʃt/ *adj.* not likely to happen, improbable, ridiculous: *He has some far-fetched ideas about building a huge company in only a year's time.*

fulfillment /fʊlˈfilmənt/ *n.* performance or completion of something: *The fulfillment of obligations under the contract will take two years.*

harness /ˈhɑːrnɪs/ *v.* to capture the power of something: *When we built a dam across the river, we harnessed the river's power to produce electricity.*

pioneer /ˌpaɪəˈnɪr/ *n.* a person who leads the way for others into a new area of knowledge or invention: *He was a pioneer in computer science.*

veracity /vəˈræsəti/ *n.* truthfulness: *I do not doubt his veracity.*

Unit 9
Chapter 1

dilemma /diˈlemə/ *n.* a difficult choice between two (usually undesirable) alternatives, a quandary: *She was in a dilemma over staying in her tiny apartment or taking the time and trouble to move.*

elect /ɪˈlekt/ *v.* to choose, to decide: *The student elected to attend a university in Germany.*

give-and-take /ɡɪv ən teɪk/ *phr. n.* willingness of people on both sides to listen to each other and to accept (some of) the other's wishes or opinions, a compromise: *There must be give-and-take from both countries if this war is to end.*

negotiate /nɪˈɡoʊʃieɪt/ *v.* to reach an agreement through discussion: *The labor union negotiated a wage increase.*

overwhelming /ˌoʊvərˈwelmɪŋ/ *adj.* overpowering: *The stench from the rotten eggs was overwhelming.*

prime /praɪm/ *adj.* main, greatest: *Her prime concern now is finding another job.*

self-esteem /self ɪˈstiːm/ *n.* a feeling of liking oneself, a sense of self-worth: *When she got a better job, her self-esteem improved.*

sibling /ˈsɪblɪŋ/ *n.* a person with the same parents as someone else, a brother or sister: *I have two siblings: my brother and my sister.*

stigma /ˈstɪɡmə/ *n.* a mark of shame or disgrace: *His father was a criminal, and that has been a stigma all his life.*

Chapter 2

breadwinner /ˈbredwɪnər/ *n.* a person who works to support others: *She is a breadwinner who supports two children.*

concession /kənˈseʃn/ *n.* a special demand by someone: *To sell our house, we made a concession to the buyer by agreeing to put on a new roof.*

dedication /ˌdedɪˈkeɪʃn/ *n.* personal devotion, commitment to something: *That doctor has great dedication to her work.*

discrimination /dɪˌskrɪmɪˈneɪʃn/ *n.* unfair treatment, especially because of race, sex, age, religion, etc.: *There is much racial discrimination in the world.*

juvenile /ˈʤuːvənl/ *n.* a youth or child, especially one under the age of 16: *Juveniles must have an adult to take care of them.*

priority /praɪˈɔːrəti/ *n.* the tasks or beliefs that are most important and require attention: *His priorities include working at his job, studying for his classes, and keeping his girlfriend happy.*

reap /riːp/ *v.* to cut down and collect, to harvest: *In the fall, farmers reap their crops.*

reluctant /rɪˈlʌktənt/ *adj.* hesitant: *He is reluctant to spend much money, because he thinks he may lose his job.*

sue /suː/ *v.* to file a lawsuit, to make a claim in court that one's legal rights have been violated by others, that they should be protected or restored, and that the others should pay for one's suffering and damages: *She sued the company because it was unfair to women and racial minorities.*

Unit 10
Chapter 1

competent /ˈkɒmpɪtənt/ *adj.* having the ability to do something well, having good or excellent skills: *She is competent in accounting; he is a competent manager.*

disgruntled /dɪsˈɡrʌntld/ *adj.* discontented and dissatisfied: *He is disgruntled about not receiving an increase in pay.*

escalating /ˈeskəleɪtɪŋ/ *adj.* increasing: *How are we going to keep up with the escalating costs of things?*

interaction /ˌɪntərˈækʃn/ *n.* communication with someone through conversation, looks, or action: *He doesn't have much interaction with his parents.*

miss out on /mɪs aʊt ɒn/ *phr. v.* not to participate in something, not enjoy: *Be sure to come to the picnic because if you don't, you will miss out on the fun.*

motivate /ˈmoʊtɪveɪt/ *v.* to give a reason to do something: *A desire to go to medical school motivates her to study hard every day.*

radical /ˈrædɪkl/ *adj.* very unusual, different from what is normal: *We noticed a radical difference in our son's behavior after he finished college and got a job.*

restore /rɪˈstɔːr/ *v.* to renew, to refresh: *A long stay at the hospital restored her health.*

secure /səˈkjʊər/ *adj.* protected from danger or harm: *He feels secure in the locked apartment.*

Chapter 2

is bound to /ɪz baʊnd tuː/ *phr. v.* is likely to: *You are bound to fail if you don't study for your exams.*

elaboration /ɪˌlæbəˈreɪʃn/ *n.* the act of explaining or giving more details: *We need more elaboration on this matter.*

give rise to /ˈgɪv raɪz tuː/ *phr. v.* to cause to happen: *Electricity gave rise to the electronic age of computers, TVs, and telephones.*

inhibition /ˌɪnhɪˈbɪʃn/ *n.* something that makes a certain behavior difficult, usually psychologically: *He has so many inhibitions about his body that he went on a strict diet.*

intonation /ˌɪntəˈneɪʃn/ *n.* the level of the voice (high or low): *Even though they both speak English, their intonation is different, because Mary comes from London and Gina comes from New York.*

phase /feɪz/ *n.* a period of time within a longer process of change, a stage of development: *The time you spend in high school is an important phase of your education.*

recite /rɪˈsaɪt/ *v.* to speak something one knows from

memory: *The child recited his prayers before going to bed.*

state /steɪt/ *n.* a situation or position, physical, mental, or emotional: *She has cancer, so the state of her health is bad.*

suggestible /səgˈdʒestəbl/ *adj.* easily swayed or influenced: *He was new to this country and very suggestible.*

Unit 11
Chapter 1

definitive /dɪˈfɪnətɪv/ *adj.* clear and leaving no further question: *I received a definitive answer to my question.*

extraordinary /ɪkˈstrɔːrdəneri/ *adj.* outstanding, wonderful: *The violinist gave an extraordinary performance.*

fade away /feɪd əˈweɪ/ *v.* to disappear: *The scar on her arm will fade away in time.*

finite /ˈfaɪnaɪt/ *adj.* limited in number (quantity, availability), countable: *The company has finite resources that must be divided among a limited number of projects.*

recollect /ˌrekəˈlekt/ *v.* to remember, to recall: *He recollected what we had talked about yesterday, and we came to an agreement.*

retention /rɪˈtenʃn/ *n.* ability to keep or retain something: *Retention of students in that high school is low; only 50 percent of the students finish the 12th grade.*

retrieve /rɪˈtriːv/ *v.* to get something back, to rescue it, to reclaim it: *His watch fell into the water, but he retrieved it with a fishing pole.*

sufficient /səˈfɪʃnt/ *adj.* adequate, satisfactory: *We have a sufficient supply of goods on hand now.*

transform /trænsˈfɔːrm/ *v.* to change from one shape or appearance to another: *Remodeling transformed an old, dark house into a cheerful one.*

Chapter 2

absorb /əbˈsɔːrb/ *v.* to learn and remember: *She absorbs new ideas very quickly.*

deposit /dɪˈpɒzɪt/ *v.* to place valuables for safekeeping: *to deposit jewelry in a safe, to deposit your children with a baby sitter*

enhance /ɪnˈhæns/ *v.* to improve, to add to: *She enhanced the value of her house by painting it.*

feasible /ˈfiːzəbl/ *adj.* workable, possible: *Your work plan is feasible, so we can build the bridge immediately.*

landmark /ˈlændmɑːrk/ *n.* something easily seen, such as a tall building or mountain: *The tallest mountain in the area is a famous landmark.*

link /lɪŋk/ *v.* to connect: *Workers linked the railroad cars together.*

tremendous /trɛˈmɛndəs/ *adj.* huge, vast: *A landslide left a tremendous pile of rocks on the road.*

visualize /ˈvɪdʒuəlaɪz/ *v.* to picture something in the mind, to imagine: *When it snows, I like to visualize a vacation on a warm, sunny beach.*

vivid /ˈvɪvɪd/ *adj.* easy to see or imagine, clear, intense: *The reporter wrote a vivid story about the disaster.*

Unit 12
Chapter 1

committed /kəˈmɪtɪd/ *adj.* bound or obligated: *She is committed to working hard for her family.*

debut /deɪˈbjuː/ *v.* to appear for the first time, especially a play, film, or artist: *The actress debuted on Broadway last year.*

extensive /ɪkˈstɛnsɪv/ *adj.* great in amount or area, considerable: *She has extensive knowledge of Chinese history.*

feel sorry for /fiːl ˈsɒːri fər/ *phr.* to feel sad for, to pity: *I feel sorry for the people who have lost their homes in the fire.*

injustice /ɪnˈdʒʌstɪs/ *n.* an unfair thing, a broken law: *During the Civil War, many fought against the injustice of slavery.*

oppress /əˈprɛs/ *v.* to govern or treat cruelly and unjustly, to subjugate: *The upper classes oppress the poorer people by taking land away from them.*

rival /ˈraɪvl/ *n.* someone who wants to get something and keep someone else from getting it, a competitor: *Two men are rivals for the love of a beautiful woman.*

self-effacing /sɛlf ɪˈfeɪsɪŋ/ *adj.* modest, not standing out: *He behaves in a self-effacing way because he doesn't want to draw attention to himself.*

update /ʌpˈdeɪt/ *v.* to make something current or up-to-date: *The TV updated a news story on the bad storm coming to our area.*

Chapter 2

conquest /ˈkɒŋkwɛst/ *n.* a military victory: *the Roman conquest of Gaul (early France)*

content /ˈkɒntɛnt/ *n.* the ideas or meanings expressed in a speech or piece of writing, subject matter, substance: *The teacher returned his paper and said the content was not very interesting.*

dialogue /ˈdaɪəlɔːg/ *n.* a conversation between people in a book, play, etc.: *You should read this story; the dialogue is very funny.*

fault /fɔːlt/ *n.* a weak point in someone's character, a shortcoming, a foible: *He has some faults, such as sometimes talking too much.*

for short /fɔːr ʃɔːrt/ *phr. adj.* abbreviated: *Call me Bob, for short.*

in doubt /ɪn daʊt/ *phr. adj.* uncertain about someone or something: *He was never in doubt about his plans for college.*

mature /məˈtʃʊər/ *adj.* adult, fully grown: *There are mature oak trees on each side of our street.*

periodically /ˌpɪriˈɑːdɪkli/ *adv.* occurring at time intervals: *This magazine is published periodically.*

publication /ˌpʌblɪˈkeɪʃn/ *n.* book, magazine, newspaper, etc.: *She reads all the publications in the field of medicine.*

- Calgary
- Vancouver
- Seattle
- Glacier National Park
- Yellowstone National Park
- Montréal
- Ottawa
- Toronto
- Boston
- Chicago
- New York
- Philadelphia
- Washington D.C.
- West Virginia
- San Francisco
- Las Vegas
- Los Angeles
- Santa Fe
- Atlanta
- San Diego
- New Orleans
- Everglades
- Florida Keys
- Atlantic Ocean
- Mexico City
- Havana
- Kingston
- San Juan
- San José
- Panamá
- Caracas
- Bogotá
- Pacific Ocean
- Quito
- Lima
- Nazca Desert
- La Paz
- Brasília
- Easter Island
- Rio de Janeiro
- São Paulo
- Asunción
- Santiago
- Montevideo
- Buenos Aires

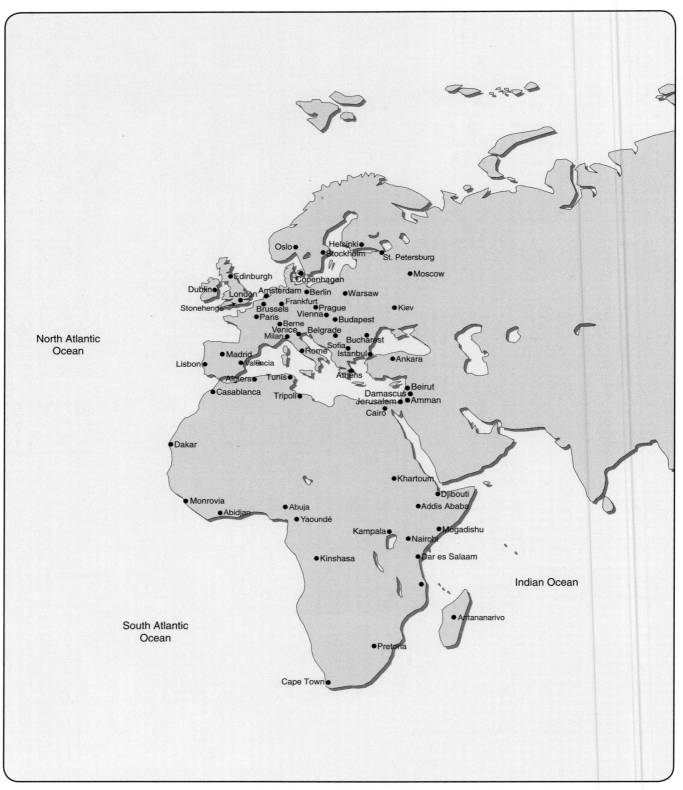

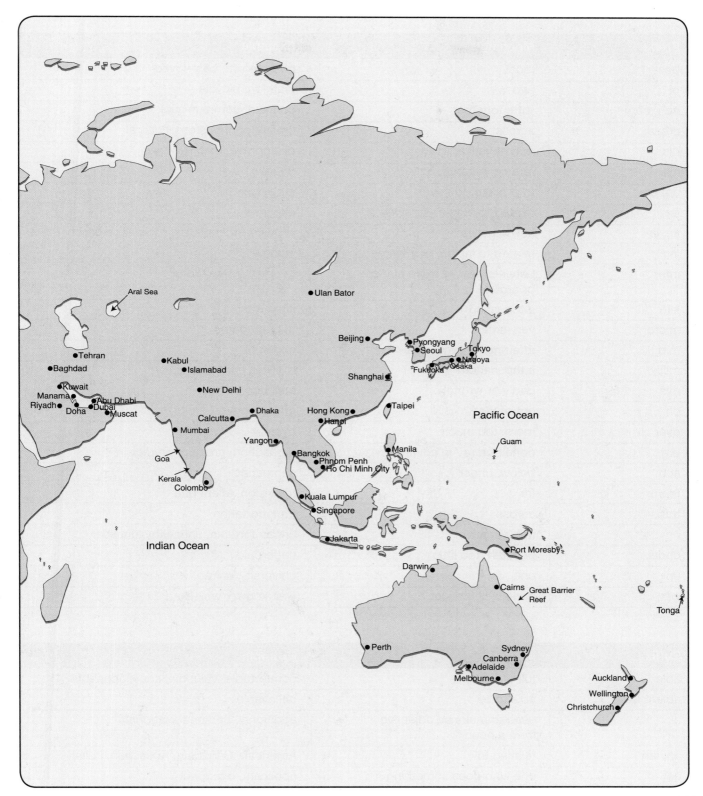

Aral Sea

●Ulan Bator

●Tehran

●Baghdad

Beijing●

Pyongyang●
●Seoul

Tokyo●
●Nagoya
Osaka●

●Kabul
●Islamabad

Fukuoka

Shanghai●

●Kuwait
Manama●
Riyadh● ●Abu Dhabi
  Doha●●Dubai
      ●Muscat

●New Delhi

Calcutta● ●Dhaka

Hong Kong●
●Hanoi

Taipei●

Pacific Ocean

●Mumbai

Yangon●

Guam

Goa

Bangkok●
●Phnom Penh
●Ho Chi Minh City

●Manila

Kerala
Colombo●

Kuala Lumpur●
●Singapore

Indian Ocean

Jakarta●

Port Moresby●

Darwin●

Great Barrier
Reef

Cairns●

Tonga

●Perth

Sydney●
Canberra●
●Adelaide
Melbourne●

Auckland●

Wellington●

Christchurch●

Prefixes and Suffixes

Here is a list of prefixes and suffixes that appear in the reading passages of this book.

Prefix	Meaning	Example
best-	most	best-known, best-loved
bi	two	biathlon, bicycle
con, com	with, together	connect, communicate
cross-	across	cross-country, cross-cultural
dis	not, negative, apart	disapprove, disorder
de	reduce, remove, not	deprive
en, em	to put into, to cover	endangered
ex	related to outside or away	expense
im, in	not, negative	impolite, independent, insensitive, inconsistent
in	related to inside, or inwards	income
inter	between two or more places or groups	Internet, international
kilo	a thousand	kilometer
micro	very small	microphone
mid	referring to the middle	midnight
milli	a thousandth	milliliter, millimeter
mis	badly or wrongly	misunderstood
off	out of, not	off-season, off-limits
over	more, too much	overeat
pre	done before / in advance	precaution, prepaid, predict
sub	below, under	submarine
tele	far	television, telephone
trans	across	transportation
un	not, negative	uncomfortable, unhealthy, unusual
under	beneath, too little	underpaid
uni	one	university, united
well-	done well, or a lot	well-known, well-liked

Suffix	Meaning	Example
able	full of	comfortable, valuable, knowledgeable
able/ible	able to be	believable
al	used to make an adjective from a noun	additional, personal, national
an, ian	relating to	American, Canadian, Australian, Italian
ant	one who does something	applicant, occupant

Suffix	Meaning	Example
ant/ent	indicating an adjective	important, independent
ate	used to make a verb from a noun	originate
ation/ution/ition	used to make a noun from a verb	combination, resolution, competition
dom	state of being	freedom
eer	one who does something	engineer
en	used to form verbs meaning to increase a quality	harden, threaten, frighten
ence	added to some adjectives to make a noun	excellence
ent	used to make an adjective from a verb	excellent
ent	one who does something	student
er, or	someone or something that does something	computer, air conditioner, ringer, reporter, competitor, learner, teacher
er	(after an adjective) more	faster, safer
ese	relating to	Taiwanese, Japanese
est	(after an adjective) most	closest, earliest, thinnest
ever	any	whatever
ful	filled with	harmful, useful, beautiful, colorful, forgetful
hood	state or condition	adulthood, childhood
ion, sion, tion	indicating a noun	permission, discussion, education, invention
ine	indicating a verb	combine
ish	relating to	British, Irish, foolish
ist	one who does something	terrorist
ity	used to make a noun from an adjective	personality, celebrity
ive	indicating an adjective	expensive, sensitive
ize	used to make a verb from an adjective	socialize
less	without, not having	hopeless
logy	the study of	biology, psychology, geology
ly	used to form an adverb from an adjective	carefully, frequently
mate	companion	roommate, classmate
ment	used to make a noun from a verb	movement, excitement, government
ness	used to make a noun from an adjective	foolishness
ous, ious	relating to	adventurous, dangerous, delicious, curious
-shaped	in the shape of	moon-shaped
some	full of	awesome, handsome
th	indicating an order	fifteenth, eighteenth
un	not, negative	unhealthy, unfortunate
ure	indicating some nouns	culture, temperature, candidature
y	indicating an adjective	healthy, flashy

Reading Rate Chart

Time (minutes)	Review Reading								Rate (words per minute)
	1	2	3	4	5	6	7	8	
1:00									600
1:15									480
1:30									400
1:45									342
2:00									300
2:15									266
2:30									240
2:45									218
3:00									200
3:15									184
3:30									171
3:45									160
4:00									150
4:15									141
4:30									133
4:45									126
5:00									120
5:15									114
5:30									109
5:45									104
6:00									100
6:15									96
6:30									92
6:45									88
7:00									85
7:15									82
7:30									80
7:45									77
8:00									75
8:15									72
8:30									70
8:45									68
9:00									66
9:15									64
9:30									63
9:45									61
10:00									60

Reading Comprehension Chart

Score	Review Reading							
	1	2	3	4	5	6	7	8
7								
6								
5								
4								
3								
2								
1								
0								